Hooves and Horns,
Fins and Feathers:

DRAMA CURRICULUM FOR
KINDERGARTEN AND FIRST GRADE

by Pamela Gerke and Helen Landalf

YOUNG ACTORS SERIES

SK
A Smith and Kraus Book

A Smith and Kraus Book
Published by Smith and Kraus, Inc.
PO Box 127, Lyme, NH 03768

Copyright ©1999 by Pamela Gerke and Helen Landalf
All rights reserved
Manufactured in the United States of America

First Edition: April 1999
10 9 8 7 6 5 4 3 2 1

Cover and Book Design by Julia Hill Gignoux, Freedom Hill Design

The Library of Congress Cataloging-In-Publication Data
Gerke, Pamela.
Hooves and Horns, fins and feathers: drama curriculum for kindergarten and first grade / by Pamela Gerke and Helen Landalf. —1st ed.
p. cm. — (Young actors series)
Discography: p.
Includes bibliographical references.
ISBN 1-57525-121-3
1. Drama in education. 2. Drama Study and teacying (primary)
I. Landalf, Helen. II. Title. III. Series: Young actor series.
PN3171.G36   1999
342.66'043—dc21   99-25281
CIP

ACKNOWLEDGMENTS

We would like to acknowledge the following drama specialists who shared their work and philosophies with us: Susan Anderson, Kathleen Edwards, Don Fleming, Jillian Jorgenson, Stacia Keogh, Barb Lachman, Michelle Landergott, Dr. Barbara McKean, David Miller, Sam Sebesta, and Ted Sod. We would also like to thank Sam Sebesta for reviewing our section "Drama and Literature," Leisa Smith for reviewing and testing some of our lessons, Susan Anderson for her guidance and the loan of her resource books, and Dr. Barbara McKean for reviewing our introductory chapters. Thank you to L.E. McCullough for granting us permission to include his play *How the People Got Fire*. Thank you to Dane Paul Bishofsky for sharing his knowledge of wild animals.

We would like to thank authors Norah Morgan and Juliana Saxton for their excellent book *Teaching Drama*, and Betty Jane Wagner for her inspiring book *Dorothy Heathcote: Drama as a Learning Medium*, both of which were highly influential in the conception of this curriculum.

Thank you to our book designer Julia Hill Gignoux, and to Marisa Smith, Eric Kraus, and the staff at Smith and Kraus, Inc. for their help and support in creating this book.

This book is dedicated to the memory of Robert Shope, a Kindergarten teacher who was a positive influence on many young lives, and to all teachers everywhere who pass the torch of creativity and caring to future generations.

Contents

PART I: DRAMA IN THE CLASSROOM

CHAPTER ONE: WHY DRAMA IN THE CLASSROOM?

CHAPTER TWO: THE CLASSROOM TEACHER AS DRAMA INSTRUCTOR

CHAPTER THREE: HOW TO USE THIS CURRICULUM

CHAPTER FOUR: MANAGING DRAMA ACTIVITIES IN THE CLASSROOM

CHAPTER FIVE: CONNECTING DRAMA TO OTHER AREAS OF CURRICULUM

CHAPTER SIX: STARTING OUT: CREATING A CONTEXT

PART II: PREPARING OBSERVATIONAL SKILLS FOR *THE JOURNEY*

LESSON 1: LOOKING AND LISTENING

LESSON 2: LOOKING, LISTENING, AND IMAGINING

PART III: PREPARING SURVIVAL SKILLS AND GEAR FOR *THE JOURNEY*

PART IV: ROLE DRAMA *THE JOURNEY*

PART V: INTERPRETING, RECORDING, AND PRESENTING *THE JOURNEY*

PART VI: NEW PERSPECTIVES

PART VII: DRAMA AND LITERATURE

PART VIII: PLAY PRODUCTION
HOW THE PEOPLE GOT FIRE

THE SCRIPT

Introduction
BY HELEN LANDALF

When I was a young girl, I once spent several weeks constantly peering from under my right hand, as if I were shading my eyes from the sun. Concerned, my teacher asked me if my eyes were bothering me. "No," I replied, "I'm Jack looking down from the Beanstalk."

During another period I was convinced that I was Dorothy in *The Wizard of Oz,* and I stopped at every street corner to sing "Somewhere Over the Rainbow."

The ease with which I could slip from one imaginary character or situation to another was almost magical. It felt completely logical to believe that the tree in our backyard was a rocket ship, or that there was a monster under the bed. As an adult, I see the same ability and desire to create an imaginary world in almost every child I come into contact with. Dramatic play is both natural and fundamental to child development, so as a teacher I find that using a child's inborn urge to imagine and play out fantasies is the most effective way to motivate and engage them in learning.

The skills of imagining and expressing seemed so simple and natural — until I was asked, along with my co-author Pamela Gerke, to write this drama curriculum for elementary teachers. Suddenly, I became almost overwhelmed with the complexity of choices that needed to be made about how to present drama to children in a way that would preserve their innate desire to imagine, yet would encourage them to strive for ever higher levels of personal and artistic excellence.

One of the first and most difficult decisions that Pamela and I needed to make was whether we would approach drama education from a performance orientation — giving children the skills necessary for the performance of scenes and plays — or a creative dramatics orientation that was as much concerned with the development of the whole child as with specific drama skills. Although some drama educators believe quite dogmatically that only one of these approaches to children's drama is the "correct" one, Pamela and I share the view that both approaches are important and valid. What was imperative, we both felt, was to present each approach with a focus on the students' process rather than on an audience-oriented product. Our quest became to create a curriculum that would integrate both creative dramatics and theater, yet keep the focus throughout squarely on the creative experience and personal development of the child.

The answer to our dilemma came with our introduction to the work of British drama educator Dorothy Heathcote. Through reading about her methods, talking with teachers who have studied with her and used her approach, and seeing her in action on film, we came to realize that her way of teaching drama was broad enough and deep enough to contain all of the goals we wished to cover in our curriculum. The study of her philosophy led us to the idea of creating an imaginary context or framework within which we could present a multitude of drama experiences.

We hope that using *Hooves and Horns, Fins and Feathers,* the K–1 Drama Curriculum, will be a unique and enjoyable experience for you and your students. We intend this curriculum to serve as a *method* for implementing drama education in elementary classrooms — one that you can follow page by page throughout the year — as well as a *model* that you can use to create drama lessons of your own, based on this example of a contextually based drama curriculum. Feel free to use the curriculum exactly as we have written it or use it as a starting point for making drama a learning medium for other subject areas as well.

In closing, Pamela and I would like to express the gratitude and admiration that we feel for all who enter the vital profession of being teachers of our children. There is certainly no career as challenging — or as rewarding — and certainly none that makes a greater impact on the future of our world.

Part I
DRAMA IN THE CLASSROOM

Chapter One
WHY DRAMA IN THE CLASSROOM?

From Creative Dramatics to Theater: A Continuum of Learning

The first-graders tiptoe into their classroom. "Shhh...," says their teacher. "We don't want to disturb the animals of the rain forest." "Look!" yells Bobby, pointing toward the coat closet. "Cobra! Ahhh!!!" He pantomimes being choked by a giant snake. The class, used to Bobby's antics, ignores him.

Marian looks down at the floor and freezes. "Jaguar tracks!" she hisses, pointing to the old stains on the carpet in the reading corner. The rest of the class comes over and stares at the stains. "Can you tell how big the jaguar is by its paw prints?" asks the teacher. "Giant!" cries one child. "It's coming to get me!" screams Bobby, who dives under a desk, followed by three other students.

"Don't be silly," Marian says, in her practical tone. "It's obviously a baby." "What do you think, Kyle?" asks the teacher, turning toward the quiet boy at the edge of the group around the carpet stains. Kyle smiles shyly, gets a ruler out of his desk and starts measuring the stains. Several other students run and grab their rulers and excitedly start measuring all the stains on the classroom carpet.

"We need to make a decision," says the teacher. "Should we stay here and try to learn more about the cat that made these tracks or should we continue on to our camp? Remember, we only have two hours until nightfall."

Across the hall in Room 6, the students of Kindergarten 1B rehearse their play. "Places for Scene One!" calls their teacher and everyone scurries to their places for the beginning of *The Adventures of Anansi*. One student wanders around, unsure where to go until her teacher reminds her that The Villagers stand next to the blackboard.

Tasha begins to read: "'How Anansi Got A Thin Waist.' Long ago in West Africa, Anansi the Spider did not look like he does today." "Excuse me, Tasha," says the teacher. "You'll have to speak much louder so that the audience to hear you. Continue, please."

Tasha reads with a tiny bit more volume: "Back then he was big all over and his waistline was very fat." Max enters the classroom from the hallway, with two pillows tied around his waist with a piece of rope. The other students, at various stations around the room, begin to giggle. The teacher chuckles, "Anansi is a pretty funny character." "He's the Trickster!" cries Sara, remembering what her teacher has said about this classic folklore figure. "Yes," says the teacher. "Now who can tell us why it's not okay to laugh and talk from backstage during the performance?"

One student calls out, "Because then the audience can't hear the play!" Another adds, "And they won't pay attention!" "That's right," says the teacher. "Now, let's continue."

In the two scenarios above, both classes are engaged in drama education in the classroom. The first example, where students are improvising an imaginary journey through the rain forest, is of a type of drama called *creative dramatics*. Creative dramatics is a general term referring to a type of activity in which participants create scenes or stories with improvised dialogue and action. It is a "process-centered form of theatre in which participants are guided by a leader to imagine, enact, and reflect upon human experiences" (The Childrens Theatre Association of America). Although creative dramatics can be presented to others, usually in the form of a demonstration, its goal is the personal development of the participants rather than the satisfaction of an audience.

The second example is of a class engaged in the art of *theater*: preparing a performance in which a script is used and in which the purpose is to communicate the story effectively to an audience. In a theater experience, performers gain skills related to communicating their artistic work to others and are able to evaluate the effects of their words and actions; however, the satisfaction of the audience is the goal. To put it simply, creative dramatics is for *the participant* and theater is for *the audience*.

Below is a visual image of the spectrum of drama activities possible with kindergartners and first graders (thanks to Dr. Barbara McKean). Although we have sequenced the lessons in this curriculum as (roughly) progressing from the left to the right on this spectrum, any or all of these activities can be used at any time with kindergarten and first-grade students. None of the activities on this spectrum are more important for children's development than any of the others: Children can benefit as much from performing in scripted play productions as they can from participating in creative play activities. The key to being an effective teacher of drama is in identifying which of the activities on this spectrum best suits your own personal teaching style and effectively addresses the needs of your students.

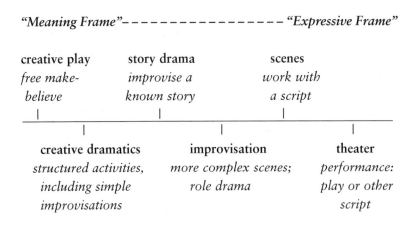

Developing Skills in a Dramatic Context

Hooves and Horns, Fins and Feathers covers the entire spectrum illustrated on the preceding page, as appropriate for kindergarten and first-grade students. This drama curriculum has at its core a technique called *role drama,* also known as *contextual drama.* This is an umbrella strategy that lays out an overall context for exploring curricular subjects via drama. The curricular subject explored in this book is, in fact, drama itself; however, role dramas can be used to pique students' interest and motivate exploration in other academic areas as well.

Within the context presented in this book, students explore a variety of drama strategies including: games, exercises, movement activities, pantomime, and dramatic play, as well as the sharing of their skills and the results of their drama lessons in public presentations. In the final sections of this curriculum, we extend the dramatic context over a range of activities centering on the interpretation and dramatization of literature and the performance of a scripted play.

Dorothy Heathcote, one of the pioneers of role drama (known as "educational drama" in Great Britain and Canada) refers to this type of drama experience as "a conscious employment of the elements of drama to educate — to literally bring out what children already know but don't yet know they know." (Betty Jane Wagner, *Dorothy Heathcote / Drama as a Learning Medium*).

The theme of *Hooves and Horns, Fins and Feathers* is the study of animals. The context of this curriculum supposes that students are a group of nature photographers who are on assignment for the Sierra Club. Through activities that develop drama skills, students prepare for and experience an imaginary journey to observe animals in the wild, create records of that experience, prepare a Time Capsule, and travel to the future. Students then continue developing their drama skills by exploring and interpreting a variety of children's literature about animals and preparing a play performance of a Native American story (of Maidu origin) in which animals are central characters. Teachers are encouraged to extend this dramatic context to other areas of the curriculum, including: science (animal studies), literature (animal stories), math (designing and drawing maps), and social studies (the history and culture of the Maidu people of California).

Educational and Developmental Benefits of Drama

One of the fundamental ways in which children relate to themselves and their environment is to make believe. Because imaginative play is a key factor in brain and body development in children, drama education is a valuable avenue for facilitating children's growth. Educational jargon aside, drama is a powerful teaching tool because, quite simply, it's fun for children. Drama offers a great potential for learning for it engages students' interest and curiosity, holds their attention, and serves as a powerful motivator for children to ask questions and explore new terrain.

As an art form, drama is intrinsically worthy of inclusion in the education of children for it teaches expressive use of body and language, helps develop skills in collaboration and communication, and, as in language arts, is concerned with understanding human experience and creating symbols to represent inner meaning. Drama education teaches children (and adults for that matter) to think like an actor thinks. An actor must think deeply about her or his character and intentions, understand the themes and symbolism of the dramatic work being explored, be self-disciplined and show perserverance with regard to the study and rehearsal of the work — including time lines and memorization — be concerned with communicating expressively and effectively, and work well with others.

Drama can also be employed as a learning medium to explore other subjects besides the art of drama. Drama activities can bring subject matter to life, stimulating children's curiosity and motivation to learn and providing a means for children to relate the material being presented to their own, personal experiences. ArtsConnection, an arts-in-education organization in New York City, is based on the belief that teachers who use the arts in their day-to-day classroom work "discover an ally in the arts: a disciplined way of knowing and learning that is both lively and focused, that can reveal and inspire,

and that connects students to their education in a meaningful way."
(from "Adapting Arts Processes to the Classroom," abstract).

Drama and the Multiple Intelligences

Howard Gardner, a developmental psychologist and neuropsychologist, defines intelligence as "an ability to solve a problem or to make something that's valued in at least one culture or community." In his influential book, *Frames of Mind*, Gardner identifies seven intelligences: linguistic, musical, logical-mathematical, spatial, bodily-kinesthetic, intrapersonal, and interpersonal. The lessons in this drama curriculum, covering the full spectrum of drama activities from creative dramatics to theater, engage all of these intelligences (with the exception of logical-mathematical, which is touched upon only peripherally).

Since the publication of *Frames of Mind*, Gardner has added an eighth intelligence, which he calls "naturalist": a sensitivity to the natural world and "the ability to make appropriate distinctions in the world of living entities." *Hooves and Horns, Fins and Feathers* with its theme of the study of animals, speaks to this naturalist intelligence. Gardner has also added another "half" of an intelligence that he calls "existential," the ability to deal with fundamental questions about existence, such as: Who are we? Where do we come from? The arts in general speak to this intelligence also, for they encourage curiosity and awareness of matters that are not scientifically quantifiable but that are concepts humanity has been pondering for eons.

In the following list of Skills Developed Through Drama Education, and throughout this entire book, we lay out the educational and developmental foundation for our curriculum. In addition, we want to mention here that another fundamental reason to include drama in the classroom is, quite simply, that it's good for children. The arts make us whole, healthy, and happy and connect us with the "left hand of knowing" — that unnamable source of wisdom. The arts feed our souls...and this is reason enough to include them in all of our lives.

Skills Developed Through Drama Education

The skills of benefit to children's education and development that are covered in this curriculum are in five general areas:

- Physical Development / Kinesthetic Skills
- Artistic Development / Drama and Theater Skills
- Mental Development / Thinking Skills
- Personal Development / Intrapersonal Skills
- Social Development / Interpersonal Skills

Many skills in each area overlap into the other areas. That drama activities contribute to all of these crucial areas of child development is precisely why drama is ideal for children's education. These skills should be seen as areas of potential, continual development, not as finite, quantifiable goals.

Physical Development / Kinesthetic Skills:

Use of the senses

Use of the whole body in movement

Awareness and control of body parts

Awareness and control of the body in space

Artistic Development / Drama and Theater Skills:

Expressive use of body and movement

Expressive use of voice and language

Commitment to believing in imaginary situations

Understanding and expression of character

Understanding and expression of setting (includes time, place, and situation)

Use and study of dramatic form

Story creation / playwriting

Communication with an audience

Development of discriminating perception as an audience member

Artistic collaboration (see Interpersonal Skills)

Mental Development / Thinking Skills:

Use and development of imagination and creativity

Ability to focus attention

Use and development of powers of observation and awareness of details

Use and development of flexible thinking and spontaneity

Use and development of memory

Use and development of problem-solving skills

Ability to sequence time and events

Organization and synthesis of ideas

Ability to understand and use symbols and metaphors

Personal Development / Intrapersonal Skills:

Awareness and expression of inner thoughts, feelings, and values

Development of self-esteem and confidence

Ability to assess and improve one's own work

Perseverance in a task

Development of resiliency and hope (by imagining "what can be" versus "what is")

Development of a sense of self-determination, the belief that one has the power to affect one's own destiny

Embodiment of story, myth, and archetype

Appreciation and enjoyment of the arts

Social Development / Interpersonal Skills:

Ability to follow directions

Communication (both listening and speaking)

Development of trust in and empathy for others

Collaboration and negotiation with others

Ability to give and receive constructive feedback

Public presentation: the outward expression of inner thoughts and feelings

Development of appropriate behavior as an audience member

Chapter Two
THE CLASSROOM TEACHER
AS DRAMA INSTRUCTOR

Arts in Education

That the arts play an important part in the education of children is an idea that is becoming more and more accepted in society and implemented by educational systems. Supported by numerous studies that prove that the arts aid in the physical, cognitive, social, and emotional development of children, increasing numbers of state education departments and local school districts in the United States are mandating the inclusion of the arts in their core curricula and are adopting standards for the performing and visual arts.

For the typical classroom teacher, these mandates may appear daunting. With good reason, classroom teachers may feel unqualified to teach the arts without proper training and experience. This drama curriculum is designed with the classroom teacher in mind. It is not, however, intended to replace drama specialists and artists-in-residence in schools. Professionals such as these are much needed in children's education and can never be simply replaced with a book such as this one. Yet, with proper preparation and support, elementary school classroom teachers can prove capable of teaching some of the basics of drama, as well as using drama as an entry point into other areas of the curriculum.

Support for the Teacher as Drama Instructor

Hopefully, the classroom teacher who teaches drama will have the full support of the school administration and faculty, both as fellow proponents of arts in education and in practical matters, such as ensuring that teachers have adequate space and time periods for drama activities. In addition, support by students' parents and their active participation in classroom drama activities will greatly add to the success of a drama program. Children whose parents are engaged and active in their child's learning process typically have better academic success than otherwise, and parental involvement helps to build advocacy for quality arts education in the community. We recommend that classroom teachers ask parents to get involved in drama lessons as volunteers, guest characters "in role," and audience members.

Whenever possible, classroom teachers can and should advocate for the inclusion of arts professionals in residencies at their schools. Teachers can learn best from professional artists who teach by example, lead teacher-in-service trainings, and offer other guidance and support that only someone who works in this field can provide. Investigate the funding and other support systems for bringing artists-in-residence into your school. Initiate projects with working artists — many artists are eager to share their expertise with children, given the opportunity.

Attitudes and Values

The essential principles of good drama pedagogy are the same as for teaching in general: respect for the ideas, feelings, processes, creativity, and originality of all students, and belief in the potential of all individuals to learn and grow. A classroom teacher who chooses to include drama in the curriculum must also be committed to the value of arts in education and be willing to embrace the process of creating art.

The artistic process is a continually evolving experience of experimenting and being open to inspiration. What distinguishes the arts from some of the other areas of the core curriculum is that in art there is no right and wrong, such as: "The sky can only be painted blue." In teaching the arts, there are often no quantifiable, verifiable, "right" answers. Like all good teachers, a drama instructor does not expect students to give answers that the instructor wants to hear, but rather is primarily interested in sparking students' interest and curiosity and facilitating their processes of self-discovery and creativity.

Children's drama teachers need to remain focused on the *process* of the drama activities rather than the finished *product* and should not put pressure on children to perform for the public as skilled actors. The skill level needed to perform effectively and expressively takes a lot of time and effort to develop, and it is unfair to children to expect them to achieve this level of competence in verbal and physical communication before they are ready. Building skill in communicating is, however, an important task in child development and we therefore include several opportunities in this curriculum for students to share their work with an audience. Nevertheless, the goal of children's drama education is to provide experiences that lead to the physical, mental, emotional, and social development of the child, not the achievement of a high level of professional performance skill.

In order to keep the focus of drama lessons on the educational process of students rather than on creating a final product, a drama instructor needs to respect the originality of all students and to trust them to find their own ways to express ideas and feelings. The nature of improvisation and much else in the art of drama is about trusting oneself to create spontaneously. The best drama instructors are those who establish an atmosphere in which it is safe to take risks and in which spontaneous responses are celebrated. The teacher who is supportive and positive about the contributions of all students thereby assures everyone that it is safe to "go out on a limb" creatively.

A safe climate is also created by drama teachers who engage students in decision making and creative planning, and who model constructive, positive feedback and self-evaluation. Artists must regularly evaluate their work. Drama education provides an excellent means for students to learn the self-regulating skills of assessing one's own work and learning processes, as well as discovering how to be a discriminating observer of the work of others and how to give helpful, critical feedback.

Above all, a classroom teacher who teaches drama must maintain a positive attitude, a healthy sense of humor, and a willingness to be flexible. The unexpected often happens in drama activities and teachers need to be willing to go with the flow and allow an activity to move in an entirely new, unplanned direction when inspiration strikes. A teacher who is flexible in this way truly respects the artistic process and the originality of all students. And don't forget to have some fun along the way — doing drama activities with kids is truly one of life's most joyful experiences!

Expectations, Goals, and Assessment

Teachers can and should expect their students to participate in drama activities under the same high standards they uphold for all classroom work: to come prepared, stay focused, listen and respond appropriately, contribute ideas to the group, take creative risks, and get along with others. These criteria are no different than those expected of professional artists. Artists must be self-disciplined in order to succeed. Drama education teaches the skills of self-regulation that students can then apply to other academic areas.

The first chapter, "Why Drama in the Classroom?" includes a list of the educational and developmental skills developed through drama education. This list can be used by teachers as a guide for determining educational goals for drama lessons. It can also be used to assess the progress of individual students with the objective of furthering each individual's continuing development in these areas. This list should not, however, be used as an evaluation checklist against which students are graded. Response to art is subjective and artistic achievement is not measurable in the same way that achievement in other areas can be measured. The skills we have outlined should be seen as areas of focus in the continuing education of children, not as end points of perfection.

In order to record the progress of students while using this drama curriculum, make one photocopy of the "Skills Developed by Drama Education" for each student. Write your observations of each student's progress on their sheet as a written narrative, rather than as a quantifiable evaluation.

Creating a Context: The Teacher In Role

As we mentioned in Chapter 1, this curriculum is centered around a type of drama called role drama, which establishes an overall context that connects all of the lessons. One of the most powerful methods for teaching within a role drama is the "teacher in role." In this method, the teacher participates in the drama while still monitoring the learning experiences of students. The teacher in role can effectively manage the group, guide students in making decisions about their drama, establish mood, help deepen students' belief in the drama, move students toward the teacher's educational objectives, and facilitate students' self-reflection on their experiences within the drama.

In order to determine what role to represent in a drama, teachers must clarify their goals for their students and assess the social health of their class. The role a teacher selects is determined by the point of view that will best forward the teacher's educational objectives. Each type of role offers different opportunities for facilitating the drama or managing the group. The following are classifications and examples of the kinds of roles a teacher might choose in a classroom role drama. (See *Teaching Drama* by Norah Morgan and Juliana Saxton for more in-depth analysis of teacher in role.)

AUTHORITY: For a class that is diffuse and unable to self-   regulate, or for students who are new to drama and are as yet unable to take responsibility for their own drama, a teacher might choose to take a role of authority, for example: the Professor, the Queen, or the Chief Surgeon. The role of a person with authority puts the teacher in a position of leadership, of being the "one who knows," the one who can disseminate useful information and manipulate the group as needed. In a role of authority, the teacher has high status, akin to the traditional instructive mode. (Note: "Status" here refers to the teacher's position of power in relation to her or his students and carries with it obvious implications for managing the class.)

HELPLESS: When a teacher wants to bring her or his students together in a common cause, she or he might choose a helpless role, such as an Injured or Lost Person, or a person who is needing explanation or direction. A helpless role creates the need for students to approach the teacher with compassion and guidance, and it is a very effective role for uniting students who may otherwise be divisive. The helpless role carries a low status for the teacher while it gives students a relatively high status, thereby engendering students' assumption of responsibility.

FACILITATOR: A facilitator role can be taken with a class of students who are self-sufficient and able to seek their own information while the teacher moves among them, offering suggestions and resources when requested. Typical facilitator roles include: an authority outside of the central action, for example the Chamberlain who is available as an advisor to the court; or a fringe role, such as someone who is a part of the scene and can ask questions about it, but who is neither a member of the group nor an authority figure. Examples of fringe roles might be: a Hospital Receptionist or TV reporter. A facilitator role generally carries a middle status, for in this role a teacher can extend or withdraw responsibility or authority from the students as she or he deems appropriate.

MEMBER OF THE GROUP: For a class with good social health, a teacher might choose to act as a member of the group in which students are in role, learning and making decisions alongside them. As a member, a teacher can take several possible roles. A high status role would be that of a leader who has the group's best interests in mind, such as Chief Scout or Head Archeologist. Another possible member role that is particularly useful is that of "second-in-command." This role, which carries a high to middle status, gives the teacher some authority to manipulate the drama but, unlike the first-in-command, places the teacher on a more equal footing with the group. Examples of second-in-command roles are: First Mate or Vice President. As a member of the group, the teacher can also take a role that is on the fringe of the group yet still allows the teacher to observe, comment, or participate in some way, such as: the Mascot or the Court Stenographer. A role as fringe member of the group carries a middle to low status.

Facilitating Reflection

The drama instructor in the classroom is ideally poised to help students see below the surface of actions to their deeper meaning. Through the imaginative element of drama, students' subjective feelings, experiences, and accumulated knowledge come into play. This invocation of the subjective, inner world is one of the most exciting aspects of drama in the classroom because it provides a medium that leads students to discover that they have something in common with the universal human experience and, therefore, with all that has gone before.

The teacher who is aware of this linkage between subjective feeling and dramatic form takes the opportunity, whenever possible, to lead students to reflect on the meaning of any particular moment in their drama activities. Guiding students to deepen in their understanding of their own experiences, "to find the feel of what they know," (in Dorothy Heathcote's words) brings them to greater self-awareness. It also awakens them to discover the joy of learning and the desire to know more.

In education, making the connection between one's own personal experiences and external informational material, such as books, is referred to as "cracking the code"; that is, students no longer feel separate from the material and find that learning is exciting and fun. The ability of drama to serve both as a conduit for finding universal meaning and to "crack the code" of education makes it a powerful entry into all curricular subjects. Teachers also have the opportunity to facilitate students' reflection on the broader issues of the subject of the role drama itself. For example, a drama about a visit to the zoo might engender reflection about endangered species of animals; or a drama about a family reunion might stimulate reflection about the definition of "family."

Asking Questions

In teaching drama, as in all teaching, the ability to articulate thought-provoking questions and to respond sensitively to the answers given is one of the most useful skills a teacher can develop. All teachers should prioritize developing and practicing the skill of asking questions that encourage learning and growth.

Questions asked by a teacher can be either limiting or freeing for students. Limiting questions are those in which the teacher conveys, either subtly or overtly, her or his own expectation of the "right" answer, that the student then tries to discover and deliver. In this case, question asking does not support the healthy development of children, except perhaps by honing their ability to satisfy an external authority and avoid conflict. Freeing questions, on the other hand, are those that signal to the student that one particular answer is neither expected nor desired. The teacher does not pose the question in the status of higher authority, but instead invites the student to participate as an equal in the discussion, thus freeing the student to answer honestly and without fear of retribution.

Freeing questions encourage students to develop the habit of looking at something from many perspectives because the teacher has established the concept that knowledge is not finite. Freeing questions are asked honestly, with true interest in the response, not with the implication that the teacher already knows the answer and is only seeking to find out if the student knows it as well. Statements that evoke a response can also be freeing if they are open-ended, such as statements beginning with "I wonder…" or, "I can't imagine why…" or, "You know, it seems to me…"

Teachers should be aware of their purpose in asking a particular question. Questions can be used by teachers to establish a dramatic mood, motivate a group decision, encourage shy students to contribute, stimulate students to research, or encourage insight into the significance of a dramatic experience. Asking questions can also be used by teachers to manage the class or discover information about students, such as by seeking to discover what they do or don't know or understand, or clarifying what students think or how they feel about their knowledge. A teacher's questions should be motivated by her or his educational goals for students. Well-selected questions can stimulate students to interpret their experiences, identify what is significant for them in those experiences, consider alternatives, make suppositions, or discover their personal feelings or values.

Equally important as articulating appropriate questions is the matter of how the question is posed. The teacher should be aware of word choice, tone of voice, and body language so as to not imply any expectation of a particular response. Also important is how the teacher responds to the answer given. In drama, teachers must listen respectfully to all suggestions and statements made by students, while encouraging them to consider the implications of each possibility. Teachers can point out the probable results of a specific action, thus leading students to consider the consequences of their ideas before making final decisions. When students do make a decision about their drama, the teacher must be willing to go along with their choices (as long as they do not violate the teacher's own limits for appropriate behavior). In honoring students' decisions, the teacher helps them feel a sense of ownership of the drama activity, thereby leading to greater enthusiasm and participation than if students feel they have no say in the decision-making process.

The following types of questions should be avoided: those that elicit a yes/no response and, in certain situations, those beginning with "Why?" and "How did/do you feel?" Yes/no responses don't require any real depth of thought. The question, "Why?" should be avoided with regard to personal responses. Often students don't know why they feel a certain way or why they made certain decisions (Do you?) and they may feel defensive when asked to explain. Your questions should focus on the context and essence of the experience and you should ask "Why?" only when trying to obtain factual information.

The question, "How did/do you feel?" should also be avoided as it can engender vague responses or lead students to feel that you are prying into their personal feelings. Dorothy Heathcote recommends that teachers ask questions directed at the students' *concerns,* rather than asking students what their feelings are (see Morgan and Saxton, *Teaching Drama*). For example, "What were you concerned about when you discovered that the Queen was missing?" Or, "What were your concerns when the pirates came on board?"

How to Prepare to Teach Drama

One of the best ways to prepare for doing drama activities in the classroom is to take an active interest in your own artistic development. For example: Take a drama class, participate in a community performance, go to see theater performances, read plays and books about drama. Studying and participating in any other art form besides drama, especially performing arts such as music or dance, will help you to appreciate the artistic process. In other words: DO IT!

Read books and magazines dedicated to the art of teaching drama, a number are listed in the Bibliography, and otherwise prepare yourself by learning about the philosophy and methods of teaching creative processes. Join a local or national organization for the advancement of children's drama education. For additional support and ideas talk with other teachers who do drama activities or have worked with theater artists in their classroom.

Conclusion

This chapter briefly outlines what we believe are the key points for assuming the mantle of teaching drama in the classroom. For more information about teaching drama, see the Commentary at the end of each lesson, as well as the Glossary for definitions of drama terms. We agree with Dorothy Heathcote who says that "the time has come to show all teachers, including classroom teachers, how they can use drama to achieve something that cannot be attained as effectively in any other way" (Betty Jane Wagner, *Dorothy Heathcote / Drama As A Learning Medium*). Drama is indeed a mighty force for children's education when it is used to aid in the development of the whole child, to evoke understanding and a feeling of connection to the universal human experience, to enhance creativity and aesthetics, and to stimulate curiosity, enthusiasm for learning, and joy.

Chapter Three

HOW TO USE THIS CURRICULUM

If you are like many classroom teachers, the lessons in this book may be very different from the types of activities you usually engage in with your students. Or, if you are lucky enough to be working in a school or district where teachers are supported in integrating the arts into the curriculum, this type of material may be more familiar to you. In either case this chapter will help guide you in determining how this Drama Curriculum can fit into your classroom schedule, acquaint you with how the material in the curriculum is organized, and assist you in effectively presenting the lessons in this book.

How the Drama Curriculum is Organized

Hooves and Horns, Fins and Feathers is organized around a specific imaginary context. The context supposes that the students are expert nature photographers who are sent into the wild on a mission to photograph and record the behavior of animals. This imaginary framework underlies every lesson and activity in the curriculum and acts as a motivation for students to learn and practice drama skills. Because the context is so important to the presentation of the curriculum, teachers are urged to read the entire book before beginning instruction, paying particular attention to the chapter "Starting Out: Creating the Context."

The context created for the Drama Curriculum need not be isolated to the periods set aside for Drama activities. Drama Curriculum context provides a perfect opportunity for the teacher to extend the study of animals, endangered species, photography, and survival skills to other areas of the academic curriculum throughout the year.

Both the Drama Curriculum and your academic curriculum will be enriched by relating them to this context.

Hooves and Horns, Fins and Feathers is divided into seven sections that move from creative drama (experiencing) to formal drama (presenting), from generation (creating a story) to interpretation (putting on a play from a script), and from simple to complex dramatic skills. The order of the sections of this curriculum is based on these progressions and, for this reason, we suggest you do the lessons in the order presented in this book. In saying this, we do not mean to suggest that creative drama is merely a prerequisite for formal drama, or that putting on a play is the end goal to be attained in a drama program. Each section of this curriculum contains valuable learning experiences for students, and no part of the curriculum is to be considered a means to an end. You may choose to present the sections of this curriculum in a different order, such as beginning with a production of the play *How the People Got Fire* and ending the year's drama study with the spontaneous role drama *The Journey*. However, we believe the best results for your students will be attained by using the sequence we have prescribed.

Each section of the K–1 Drama Curriculum is divided into individual lessons, lasting fifteen to forty minutes each. Most lessons contain one to three related activities. You may do all of a lesson's activities during a single drama session, or do just one or two and save the remaining activities for another day, depending on the amount of time you have. You may also choose to omit one or more activities entirely. Once an activity has been introduced you can repeat it in any subsequent session as a warm up. You are also encouraged to try one or more of the variations listed for each activity.

We suggest that you present a lesson from this K–1 Drama Curriculum approximately once a week in sessions lasting fifteen to forty minutes each. Lessons 8, 9, and 10, *The Journey*, should be presented on consecutive days. Preparing an informal presentation of the play *How the People Got Fire* will require several rehearsals per week, each lasting approximately 30–45 minutes.

Using the Drama Curriculum Lessons

Once you have familiarized yourself with the organization of the curriculum and have carefully read all the introductory chapters and lessons, you are ready to start teaching the Drama Curriculum lessons. Each lesson contains important information under the following headings:

> **Lesson Number and Title**
> **Activity Titles, Time Required**

The specific activities that make up each lesson, as well as the approximate time required to present each activity, can be found at the top of the lesson's first page. Be aware that presentation times will vary depending on your presentation style and the responses of your students.

CONTEXT

This heading tells you how this particular lesson or activity fits into the overall context of the entire curriculum. The context is written in one or two sentences that you can share with your students before beginning the lesson. Feel free to change the wording of the context statement as you feel appropriate.

SKILLS

This heading lists the major skills from the list of "Skills Developed Through Drama Education" on pages 9–11, that are introduced or developed in the course of the activity. Once a skill has been introduced, students will naturally use it in subsequent lessons, even if it is not listed under this heading. For example, if the ability to focus attention is introduced in one activity, it will be practiced in most subsequent activities, even when the major focus of those activities is on introducing new skills.

In addition to the drama skills listed for each activity, you may find that a particular lesson also provides an opportunity for you to focus on an educational goal related to another subject area. For example, you may choose to emphasize curricular material about habitats or animal behavior along with the presentation of drama skills in some lessons in Parts I, II, and III of this curriculum.

MATERIALS / PREPARATION
Under this heading are listed any specific materials or preparation steps required or suggested in order to teach the lesson, including set-up of the physical space and construction of props.

MUSICAL SUGGESTIONS
The majority of the lessons in this book can be presented without music. However, music is very motivating for children and can help students feel more involved and less self-conscious. Several lessons in this book suggest specific musical selections, but most of the lessons in which music is required or beneficial can be successfully presented using any selection from the Discography at the end of this book or music from your own collection. In general, New Age, classical, ethnic, or folk music is more conducive to creative response than is currently popular music, and instrumental music is more effective than music with lyrics.

PROCEDURE
The lesson's procedure is written as a step-by-step guide to presenting the lesson. The procedure represents one possible way to conduct the lesson. However, you are welcome and encouraged to adapt the manner of presentation to your teaching style and to the particular needs of your students. The most important thing to remember as you teach the drama lessons in this book is to maintain a flexible, nonjudgmental attitude that allows students a safe forum for freedom of self-expression.

COMMENTARY
The commentary provided at the end of each lesson or activity provides you with additional, pertinent information about how to successfully present the lesson and about the significance of the lesson in the development of dramatic skills, or in child development in general.

VARIATIONS
These are ideas on alternative ways to present the activity or ways to extend the activity to enhance learning in other areas of your curriculum.

LITERATURE SELECTIONS
The lessons in Part VII: Drama and Literature contain the text of any written selections used in the lesson. Alternative literature selections that can be used in a similar way are listed at the end of each of these lessons. All selections mentioned in the literature section and throughout the book can be found in the Bibliography.

Making Space for Drama

It is a sad truth that adequate space for drama and movement activities in the typical elementary school building is minimal. While most schools and school districts spend thousands of dollars on computer equipment, educational planners often do not consider providing adequate movement space for children in order for them to use the natural learning resource of their own bodies and imaginations. Therefore it becomes the responsibility of the classroom teacher to adjust, adapt...and advocate for change in this vital area.

Try the following suggestions to maximize space for drama activities in your classroom:

1. Create a routine for clearing as much space as possible in your classroom. Challenge students to rearrange furniture in record amounts of time (and to put it back when the lesson is over).

2. When classroom furniture must stay in place, use any open space at the front or back of your classroom for drama activities. Many activities can also incorporate students traveling up and down aisles between furniture.

3. Have only half of the class or small groups of students participate in an activity at a time with the rest of the class watching. Repeat the activity again with the other group(s) participating, or rotate giving students a turn to participate on different days.

As an alternative to presenting drama activities in the classroom, use other open spaces in your school building. Try the music room, gym, lunchroom, stage, computer lab, library, and do forth. It is also fun to do a drama activity outdoors.

Troubleshooting

Sometimes, despite your best efforts, you may find yourself in the middle of a drama activity that seems "stuck": The students just don't know what to do. In this situation, try the following:

- Give an example or demonstration of the kind of responses that are possible.
- Do only one part of a lesson instead of the entire lesson.
- Take a role in a drama that allows you to give guidance within the context of the story. (For more on this approach, as well as other hints for managing drama activities, see Chapter 4, "Managing Drama Activities in the Classroom.")
- Stop, and try again on another day!

Teacher Self-Assessment

At some point after a lesson is completed you will want to assess the effectiveness of your presentation. We suggest waiting at least an hour or two before making an assessment because by that time you will be able to be more objective and less self-critical.

First, think about what went well in the lesson. When were the students particularly engaged? What were some really creative responses you observed? At what points did you feel that they really "got" the content of the lesson?

Next, take a look at any difficulties or problems you encountered and try to determine their cause. Were your directions to students unclear? Did the students need more direction during the transitions from one part of the lesson to the next? Did you allow a student's negative behavior to garner too much of your attention? Be as specific as you can about the cause of any difficulties to help yourself avoid them in the future.

Last of all, just as you praise your students for striving for their highest potential, treat yourself well — no matter how the lesson went — for doing something that is new and challenging for you. You will find that, over time, leading your students in drama activities seems less overwhelming and will, instead, become vastly rewarding to both you and your students.

For information on assessment of students see the section on Expectations, Goals, and Assessment in Chapter 2, "The Classroom Teacher as Drama Instructor."

We hope you and your students will enjoy *Hooves and Horns, Fins and Feathers: Drama Curriculum for Kindergarten and First Grade*. We encourage you to experiment, take risks, dare to fail...and to succeed. Have fun, and revel in the growth and depth of learning that drama will bring to your classroom.

Chapter Four
MANAGING DRAMA ACTIVITIES
IN THE CLASSROOM

Many teachers, when imagining leading their students in a drama activity, envision a scene of noisy, directionless chaos. Unfortunately, the fear of such an occurrence often prevents these teachers from even attempting to do drama in their classrooms. While a misdirected drama activity can certainly lead to noisy confusion, a well-planned, well-executed lesson leads to engaged, motivated activity.

When students are engaged in drama activities, they are enthusiastic and excited, and they are actively involved with the content of the lesson and with each other. In other words, they're responding exactly the way we, as educators, should want them to respond. However, this type of active learning requires students to move about and speak to one another more than some teachers are comfortable with. The discomfort some teachers feel when faced with noisy, active learning is based on a now outdated cultural standard for student behavior that maintains that students are not learning unless they are sitting quietly at their desks. However, our current understanding of child development and learning styles tells us that the more physically and emotionally a child is involved in learning, the deeper and longer-lasting that learning will be. Thus, we have to change our idea of what learning looks like in order to embrace drama as an appropriate educational activity.

Another aspect of doing drama that may be daunting to some teachers is the fact that, in a drama lesson — particularly in role drama — students take the lead in controlling the direction of the activity. The teacher is present as a guide and facilitator rather than being completely in charge of the outcome of the lesson. This requires teachers, many of whom are accustomed to being at the helm of a learning situation, to let go of their idea of how a drama lesson "should" progress so that their students' creativity can shine through.

Just as we must teach children the rules of a game before they can play it safely and successfully, we must educate them about *how* to engage in drama activities. In most classrooms drama is not part of the usual school day. There is no reason that students in such classrooms would know how to behave during a drama lesson. But often teachers who have never introduced drama before will try it once, then give up altogether because their students did not respond in the way they expected. This is as unfair to students as it would be to give long division problems to a class that had never been introduced to long division, then say "never again" when they failed to solve the problems correctly!

This chapter will give you some general guidelines for leading your students in drama activities. Keep in mind as you read that "Practice makes perfect" and the more you use drama in your classroom the more positively and appropriately your students will respond.

Setting Clear Expectations

As in any teaching situation, it is of vital importance to set clear boundaries and expectations for behavior. It is often helpful to have your students collaborate with you in formulating a set of rules specifically for drama sessions. An example of such a set of rules might be:

Listen and follow directions.
Move carefully, touch gently.
Respect the ideas of others.
Do excellent work.

It is best to state rules in a positive frame — that is, describing what students can and should do — rather than telling students what they should not do. You may also want to set behavioral expectations specific to the space you are working in, such as "Move only on the floor of the gym and stay off the bleachers." The more clear you can be at the outset about what kind of behavior you expect the more safe your students will feel and the more positively they will respond.

It is useful to have a "freeze" signal: a signal that immediately stops all speaking and activity. A beat on a drum or tambourine works well for this purpose, as does briefly turning off the lights in the classroom. It is a good idea to set up the freeze signal at the beginning of the very first drama lesson, as we have done in Lesson 1 of this curriculum, and to give the students a chance to practice responding to it several times.

Giving Clear Directions

It is very possible for a drama activity to fail because directions were not given clearly. The lessons in this book have been written so as to facilitate your making the directions to students as clear as possible. It is important that students are always told where to go to begin a new activity and what to do when they get there. They need to be told how to engage in the activity and what to do when the activity has been completed. For suggestions on how to give directions in role, see Managing in Role, below.

The most common place for management to break down is in the transition between two sections of a lesson. For example, if the whole class does an improvisation and the students are then asked to get into partners to work on a movement activity, the transition from working as a whole class to working in partners could be problematic. (For suggestions on how to solve this problem see the section Organizing Groups.) It is important to plan exactly how the transition will take place and to communicate that plan to students.

Managing in Role

There may be many occasions when you will be able to set behavioral expectations and give directions within the context of the specific dramatic activity your students are engaged in. For example, if you wish your students to speak quietly you might, in a dramatic whisper, say "We must speak quietly or the Queen will overhear us!" Or, if you wish students to keep their movements within a certain area of the room you might say, "Remember that the campsite is surrounded by quicksand. One step past this line and you will never be seen again." Setting expectations in this way not only makes clear to students how they should behave, but it also deepens their involvement in the drama situation. Children delight in seeing their teacher play an imaginary role and often respond more willingly than they would if the teacher gave directions in her usual "authority role."

Facilitating Group Decision Making

Creative drama activities, such as those found in this curriculum, often require students to engage in group decision making. There are several ways that you, as a teacher, can facilitate the decision-making process depending upon the amount of time you wish students to spend making a decision, the relative importance of the decision itself, and your overall goal for the activity.

In making a fairly important decision, such as how a drama will begin or end or what type of problem will occur, it may be best to spend the time required for a group to come to consensus. You can help guide this process by making students aware of the implications contained in each suggestion they make. For example, if a student suggests that everyone in the drama be killed, you can point out one of the implications of that choice — that no one will be left to tell the story of what happened. Making students aware of the implications of each possible choice helps them to draw rational conclusions, often resulting in a collective agreement.

In making a less crucial decision, or in a case where a consensus cannot be reached, it is expedient to have students take a majority-rule vote. It's often best to narrow the vote to only two or three possible choices, for example: "Shall we journey by plane or by train?" Be aware that voting can sometimes lead to popularity contests or girls-against-boys battles. We recommend that, when voting, you keep students focused on how the issue under debate relates to the drama rather than allowing it to become a contest between students.

When making a relatively unimportant decision or when the group has come to an impasse, it is sometimes best to simply take the first, workable suggestion offered and move on from there. For example, if you need a name for a person in your drama you can say, "What would be a good name for this person?" If the first student's response is "Max!" and that is an appropriate name, simply say, "Okay, the name of the person is Max." Then continue on without debating the issue further or taking other suggestions.

In all situations where group decision making is required you, as the teacher, must be aware of your goal. If you want the group to feel complete ownership of a particular decision and to practice the valuable process of group collaboration, you may decide to take time for the group to examine implications of all suggested choices and come to a consensus. If your goal is for students to feel some investment in a decision but also to move the drama forward without delay, you may decide to have them take a vote. When your major goal is to keep the momentum of the activity going, it may be best to make a relatively unimportant decision yourself.

Organizing Groups

To organize students into pairs or small groups, you may find it easiest to let them quickly make their own choices by giving them a task such as "By the time I count to ten, please find a friend and touch elbows with them." Putting a time limitation on choosing groups prevents students from belaboring the process.

In some classes, due to interpersonal issues between students, asking them to choose their own partners or groups can be problematic. In this situation you may want to organize your students into appropriate groupings before the beginning of the lesson and read or post your list as part of preparing for the activity. Another possibility is to draw numbers out of a hat and allow groups to be chosen randomly.

Dividing your class in half can be accomplished simply by drawing an imaginary line through the middle of the group. Or, you may choose to have students count off by 1s and 2s to make the grouping more random. The most important thing to remember in organizing groups is that it should happen quickly and matter-of-factly rather than becoming a major focus of the lesson.

Casting Roles

A special challenge in dramatizing stories or presenting plays with students is casting roles. In casting roles for a story that the class will dramatize several times, choose volunteers for the central roles in the first playing of the story whom you know will model full, enthusiastic participation for the other students. In the second playing of the story, try casting outgoing students alongside shy or more reluctant students in the major roles. It is important to remember that the focus of dramatizing a story is the experience of the participants, not the outward appearance of the product.

When casting a play for informal production, it is best to let students choose their own roles rather than having them audition. Auditioning invites students to compare themselves with others and to focus on their limitations. If several students would like to play the same role, you can pull names from a hat to determine the final casting. Again, it is important to consider who will benefit most from playing a role rather than choosing the child who will perform it the most easily and effectively. It is crucial that the teacher model the attitude that all students are capable of dramatic expression.

Acknowledging Appropriate Behavior

One of the best ways to manage student behavior in any learning situation is to acknowledge appropriate behavior when you see it. It is just as important to praise positive behavior as it is to praise skill and creativity. Your students yearn for your attention. Once they discover that behaving appropriately is the way to get that attention, they will eagerly exhibit the behavior you seek. Comments such as "I really appreciate the way Billy is listening to my directions" or "Susan and Jesse are being very gentle with each other as they move together" lets all of your students know what kind of behavior you value.

Acknowledging appropriate behavior is most effective when it is coupled with ignoring negative behavior. Although it can be extremely difficult to ignore a student who is behaving inappropriately, it is crucial to successful classroom management. Try "catching" a difficult student behaving well — even for a second — and acknowledge him or her immediately.

Dealing with Nonparticipation

A major concern for teachers who have never tried drama activities with their class is that their students "won't do it." Our experience is that children love drama and that most will gladly participate when given an opportunity.

While most children participate in drama readily, it is not uncommon to have one or two students in a class who may initially resist joining in. Sometimes, if a child is timid or shy or comes from a family or cultural background where physical or vocal expression is not encouraged, he or she may feel threatened and overwhelmed when invited to join a drama experience. It is usually best to let such students enter the activity when they feel ready. Allow them to watch for awhile or to take on a responsibility that does not require them to perform in front of others, such as turning on lights or music during an activity. Remember that observing an activity is a form of participation, and even students who are simply watching may be deeply involved.

Another type of nonparticipation stems from a student's desire to enter into a power struggle with you or to impress his or her peers by being too "cool" to participate. In this case it is best to simply state that participation is mandatory, just as it is for any other classroom activity. Your attitude carries a lot of weight in this situation: If you value drama as much as you value the other curricular subjects, your students are more likely to do so as well.

Guiding the Reluctant Student

The reluctant student is one who participates in drama activities but does not take initiative and tries to remain in the background. It is important to allow such a student to enter the activity at his or her own pace rather than forcing them to take a more active role. You can begin to get a reluctant student involved in small, relatively non-threatening ways. An example of this can be found in *The Journey: An Example*. Annie, who has been reluctant to participate in the drama, is given the role of the victim of a tiger attack. This role does not necessarily require her to speak, but it does draw her into involvement with the story and with her peers.

Guiding the Dominating Student

The dominating student is one who aggressively seeks to control his or her classmates as well as the direction of a drama activity. The dominating student should be differentiated from the natural leader — someone who is also concerned with bringing out the best in others. The dominating student wants to "run the show," not allowing others the opportunity to express their ideas. One way to handle such a student is to give them a role that requires them to hold back: Perhaps they are the keeper of a secret that may not be divulged to others, or a powerful monarch who commands by gesturing rather than speaking. Note that in these examples the student is given a powerful role rather than a helpless one. Another approach that can be taken in a class with a dominating student is to structure activities in a way that ensures that every child will have an opportunity to contribute. For example, you might go around a circle giving each student a chance to add to a group story rather than having them call out ideas spontaneously.

Encouraging an Appropriate Sound Level

Students will naturally be more verbal when engaging in a drama activity than they are when sitting at their desks listening, reading, or writing. It is necessary and appropriate for them to speak animatedly with one another during a drama session in order to solve problems and collaborate creatively. Therefore, teachers should expect that the classroom sound level during a drama lesson will be higher than at some other times. Many students have difficulty moving their bodies, in particular, without speaking or making sounds. This is partly because the only other time they have a chance to move freely is on the playground where shouting and yelling are the norm. It is also an indicator of the strong developmental connection between the voice and the body and the naturally high energy level of children. Most students simply need training and practice in how to move about the classroom without vocalizing loudly.

It is useful to demonstrate to the class that body movement can provide ways to communicate and express oneself without the need for sound. Ask students to show you a variety of emotions using only their bodies and facial expressions. Encourage them to show the intensity of those feelings without using their voices. For example, "Show me with your body that you are excited...angry...sad...surprised." Last of all, be sure to praise your students whenever they are particularly successful in engaging in a drama lesson with an appropriate sound level.

Motivating Through Drama

Although you may find it challenging, initially, to manage drama activities with your class, over time you will find that drama becomes its own motivation. Your students will want to behave appropriately because they will want you to keep providing them with drama experiences! Letting your students know that their appreciation and enjoyment of drama activities is important to you will ultimately be your most effective management tool.

Chapter Five
CONNECTING DRAMA TO OTHER AREAS OF CURRICULUM

The major goal of this drama curriculum series is to guide teachers in introducing and developing drama skills with their students. However, drama can also be used as a highly effective tool in enhancing learning in other areas of the curriculum. This chapter will give you general suggestions in how to use drama to enliven the teaching of Language Arts, Social Studies, Mathematics, Science, Visual Art, and Music in the elementary grades. For specific ideas on integrating the lessons in this Drama Curriculum into other subject areas, see the Variations following each lesson.

Language Arts

Drama offers a rich source of opportunities for deepening and expanding the study of the language arts because both drama and language arts have in common the use of language to communicate and the utilization of character, setting, and other elements of the story form. In addition to the dramatization of poetry and stories, which is covered extensively in Part VII, drama can also be used to enhance the study of Language Arts in the following ways:

1. Movement Activities: Ask students to make the shapes of letters or spell words with their bodies. Groups of children can spell words, each child in the group forming one letter.

2. Pantomime: Have students pantomime as many things as they can think of that begin with a particular letter. If the letter were B, for example, they might pantomime playing baseball,

being bears or birds, blowing up balloons, and so on. Another pantomime activity is to have students show a verb in pantomime, such as walking, then add adverbs such as *softly, bravely, cautiously, excitedly* to the verb and ask them to change their movement accordingly.

3. Playwriting / Dramatization: Have students act out simple stories that they have written individually or as a class.

4. Spontaneous Role Drama: Use improvisational drama to expand on the historical period, setting, or theme of a piece of literature. For example, to prepare students to read or hear a story with the theme of family relationships, have them do a spontaneous role drama in which they have to find a foster family for a child from another planet, leading them to discuss what they think are the important elements of a family.

Foreign Language

Drama activities can give students a motivation for learning and practicing words and phrases in another language.

1. Role playing / Simulation: Teach students a simple phrase in a foreign language, such as "Muchas gracias" (thank you very much — Spanish). Set up an imaginary situation, such as a grocery store where students are shopping, asking questions and buying products. Each student must find at least three occasions to say "Muchas gracias" to someone else.

2. Play production: Many folktales provide natural opportunities for students to learn words, phrases, and even songs in another language. *Multicultural Plays for Children, Grades K–3* and *Grades 4–6* by Pamela Gerke contain many plays that include foreign language.

Social Studies

Engaging in drama activities is a wonderful way to expose children to other cultures and time periods because it allows them to experience being "in another person's skin." Drama enlivens the study of history by infusing past events with the students' own experiences and feelings of the present, thereby helping them realize that history is about real people who had thoughts and feelings much like their own. Drama is also a highly effective way of developing interpersonal skills.

1. Story Dramatization: Have students dramatize folktales from another culture, discussing the differences between that culture and their own.

2. Spontaneous Role Drama: Have students do a role drama that gives them an experience of an essential element of a culture or historical period. Go for a deeply felt feeling of identification rather than an accurate simulation. For example, in preparing students to learn about the American pioneers, have them imagine they are a community of people packing their wagons for a long journey, deciding what to take and what they must leave behind.

3. Improvisation: Use improvised scenarios to explore family and school relationships and to resolve classroom conflicts. An example of this might be having two students do an improvised scene in which one child tries to get the other to give her the answers to a test.

Mathematics

The actual process of solving mathematical problems requires a very different set of skills than the skills used in drama. However, drama can be used to motivate a need for mathematical calculation, as in the story problems in the examples below:

1. Spontaneous Role Drama: The need to do mathematical calculations can be built into a dramatic situation, for example: "We had five water jugs with us when we first became stranded on this desert island. Now three of the jugs are empty. How many jugs do we have left?"

2. Mantle of the Expert: Students as town planners using measurements in scale to map the town, or toy designers working out the correct measurements for the Three Bears' beds.

3. Play Production: "How many centimeters of butcher paper will we need to create a backdrop that covers the blackboard?"

Science

Integrating drama with science can be challenging because science deals with processes, systems, and verifiable facts whereas drama tends to deal more with the human experience. There are ways, however, to give students an experience of scientific phenomena through drama:

1. Movement Activities: Movement can be used to help students imagine such natural forces as gravity, states of matter, and magnetic attraction. For detailed lessons that integrate movement with earth science, see Helen Landalf's *Moving the Earth: Teaching Earth Science Through Movement in Grades 3–6*.

2. Spontaneous Role Drama: Students can explore science topics by taking an imaginary role that will motivate learning. For example in studying weather, students might take on the role of scientists who shrink themselves so they can enter droplets of water and experience evaporation and precipitation.

3. Mantle of the Expert: Create situations where students need scientific information to solve problems that they, as "experts" in a particular field, have been presented with. For example,

perhaps they are agricultural engineers who need to create an irrigation system for an imaginary village. To fulfill this role they will need to gather information on the role of water and soil in the growth of plants.

Visual Art

Drama provides opportunities for students to both practice and appreciate the visual arts.

1. Playwriting, Dramatization: Show students realistic or abstract works of art and have them create stories based on what they see. The stories could be verbalized, written, or dramatized.

2. Movement Activities: Have students create "sculptures" with their bodies, or dance their impressions of realistic or abstract works of art.

3. Play Production: Involve students in designing and constructing sets, props, and costumes for an informal play production.

Music

Music and drama make excellent companions because music evokes mood, which can find its expression in drama.

1. Movement Activities / Pantomime: Play a piece of music for students and ask them to imagine a setting, character, or situation that the music suggests to them. They could then express their ideas through movement and pantomime. For example, play short selections of music of different kinds and have students enter the playing area one at a time, walking as the character each type of music suggests to them.

2. Dramatization / Play Production: Have students use musical instruments to create sounds for a story dramatization or informal play production. They can also play live or recorded music during the transitions between scenes of a play.

Physical Education and Dance

Physical action is a major element in drama, and therefore many connections can be drawn between drama and physical education, particularly dance.

1. Movement Activities: Many of the activities in this curriculum that are geared toward the development of body awareness and movement skills can also be used in physical education or dance lessons by focusing on the movement itself rather than on the activity's dramatic context. For example, by de-emphasizing its photography context, the activity "Move and Freeze: Photography Practice" in Lesson 1 could be used to explore moving and stopping in an introductory physical education or dance lesson.

2. Pantomime: Exaggerating the movements of a pantomime can lead to the creation of a dance. Ask your students to pantomime an activity, then make their movements larger and larger until their entire bodies are involved. Playing background music will help students make the transition from pantomime to dance.

3. Play Production: Dances can be included in informal play productions. If performing a folktale from another culture, teach your students a traditional folk dance, or create your own folk-style dance to music of that culture. It is also possible to have students choreograph their own dances to perform as part of a play.

Chapter Six
STARTING OUT:
CREATING A CONTEXT

The teacher who uses this curriculum will be providing his or her students with a unique experience because these students will have the opportunity to learn and practice the skills and techniques of drama not by doing a series of unrelated exercises, but by engaging in activities within an overall dramatic context. Such an approach increases the students' motivation and involvement and gives a sense of purpose to each drama lesson. It is this sense of purpose that you, as the teacher, must help your students create before Lesson 1 even begins. Creating the context will require 2–4 class periods of approximately 15–30 minutes each, preferably occurring over consecutive days.

Hooves and Horns, Fins and Feathers: Drama Curriculum for Kindergarten and First Grade requires that students embrace the role of being expert nature photographers. In this role they will accept an invitation by the Sierra Club to journey into the wild to photograph animals so that children of the future will know about the animals that lived on earth at this time, even if many of them should become extinct. We suggest that you create this scenario by following the steps outlined on the following page.

Step 1. Setting the Stage

MATERIALS / PREPARATION:
- Photographs of wild animals of many kinds mounted on the bulletin boards
- Books with photographs of animals prominently displayed in the classroom

A few days before you plan to start using this curriculum, put photographs of wild animals on your classroom bulletin boards and have books with photographs of animals available in the room. There is no need to call attention to the photographs or books — simply let the students look at them as they choose.

Step 2. Creating Ownership

After the photographs have been up for a day or two, discuss them with the class. Begin by asking questions about "the photographer who took these pictures" such as *"Where do you think the photographer was standing to get this shot? How do you think the photographer might have felt being this close to a wolf?"* Move on to questions that ask the students to imagine what it would be like if they were nature photographers: *"If you were a nature photographer, what animals would you specialize in photographing? Where would you like to travel to take your photographs?"* After several such questions, ask *"If we were a company that specialized in nature photography, what might the name of our company be?"*

Allow the students to suggest several company names, discuss the merits of each, and decide on one that the class will adopt. This can be done through voting with a majority rule, or by discussing it until the class is able to reach consensus. It is important to facilitate this decision by discussing the implications of any suggestions students make. For example, if someone suggests the name "The Forest Photographers" you might ask, *"If we choose that name, does it mean we only photograph plants and animals in forests, and not deserts or mountains?"*

Step 3. Receiving the Challenge

MATERIALS / PREPARATION:
- Before students arrive, create a sign — either on cardboard or on the blackboard — with these words:

> *[The chosen name] Nature Photography Company*
> *Studio A*

- Photographs of animals cut from magazines, laid out on one or several tables
- Certificates of Photography Awards, taped to the wall. These need not be elaborate nor look highly authentic — simply write them with pen or markers on plain pieces of paper. Some examples:

PHOTO OF THE YEAR AWARD TO:
[The chosen name] Nature Photography Company
(Dated 5 years ago)

CERTIFICATE OF EXCELLENCE
"MOST EXCITING WILDLIFE PHOTOGRAPH"
To: *[The chosen name] Nature Photography Company*
(Dated 2 years ago)

- A copy of the letter (on the following page) on official-looking Sierra Club letterhead. You can make this by creating letterhead at the top of a piece of paper with your computer or by cutting a Sierra Club logo from a magazine and pasting it to the top of the paper, then photocopying the letter and pasting it below the letterhead. (Also feel free to write your own letter if you choose, as long as it covers the points in the sample letter. You are also welcome to refer to an organization other than the Sierra Club.)

Dear _____ (name of company):

As you know, many of the beautiful animals in our world are becoming extinct. There are many animals alive today that may not remain on earth for much longer. It is for this reason that we at the Sierra Club are writing to you.

It has come to our attention that _____(name of company) has been a leader in nature photography for the past twenty years. The Sierra Club would like to invite the members of your company to journey to the natural habitat of your choice to observe and photograph animals in the wild. When you return, we ask that you create a Time Capsule: a box filled with photographs, stories, drawings, models — anything that will help the children of the future learn about the animals we have today. Our hope is that children of the future will find the Time Capsule and learn about the wonderful creatures living on earth at this time.

Please reply to our request as soon as possible, as your company is our top choice for the project.

Sincerely,
Deborah Mitchell,
Special Projects Coordinator

When students arrive (such as after a recess), immediately assume your role as the Company Secretary. This is a role that will allow you to offer assistance to the photographers without being their boss — it will be more empowering to students if you are not in a role of high authority. (You can also choose another role with a similar stance, such as a Receptionist or Clerk.) Say something to students to signal to them that they are now in the world of the Photography Company, for example:

> "Welcome back, photographers! While you were out on your coffee break, the order for those new photographs arrived. Oh, and UPS came with the shipment of film. I put it in the storeroom. Also, we need to get started sorting through our latest set of photos."

Gather students at the table(s) where the photographs of animals cut from magazines have been placed. Ask students to begin sorting them into piles by categories such as: wild animals, pets, work animals, sea creatures. (Create your own categories in response to the pictures you have cut out and the knowledge level of your class.) This simple yet purposeful task should be approached with an attitude of focused, businesslike expertise.

As you guide students in their sorting task, continue interacting with them in your role as the Company Secretary. You do not need to be an actor when "in role" — it's enough for you to convey the attitudes appropriate to your role as Company Secretary (or whatever role you choose). It's perfectly all right for you to come "out of role" at any time to explain matters to students as their teacher — students will have no problem transitioning between the real world and the imaginary world of this business enterprise.

Establish the fact that your company has a long history of success and expertise by posting the award certificates and by making such statements as, *"This is how we've always done it"* or *"In all these years of business, I don't think we've ever had this kind of an order before."*

When students have been working on their sorting task for ten to fifteen minutes, announce that a letter from the Sierra Club has just arrived in the mail, and that you would like to call a staff meeting to discuss it. Ask students to be seated and read them the letter.

Step 4. Discussing the Proposal

After reading this letter to your students, discuss its contents with them as if they were members of the nature photography company. During this discussion the students will be "trying on" their new roles as company members. Some possible questions for discussion are: Do we have time to take on this project as well as keep up with our other work? Do we have the experience it takes to do this job well? Is the project of interest to the company, and why? Guide students in discussing the implications of accepting the proposal.

Although it is almost certain that most of your students will be highly enthusiastic about taking on the Sierra Club project, some of your students may be resistant to the idea, or wonder if the letter is "real." At no time during this curriculum will you attempt to fool your students into believing something that isn't true. Always be candid in answering their questions as to whether a situation is "real." In this case, respond by telling them frankly that you wrote the letter, then ask *"Are you willing to believe that it's real?"*

Being willing to believe in a make-believe situation is at the core of all dramatic experience. By being willing to believe in a situation, a place, a character, or an event, students open themselves to becoming physically and emotionally involved in the imaginary circumstance, thus making available all of the learning, reflection and growth that it has to offer.

As vital as the belief of the participants may be, it is fine to begin the curriculum even if every student is not completely committed to believing in the context of themselves as Nature Photographers: This commitment will increase over time, and opportunities to strengthen belief in the context have been built into the curriculum's lessons and activities. It is enough, for the moment, to have a majority of the students willing to go along with the dramatic context you have presented to them.

Once the photography company has accepted the proposal, discuss with your students (as company members) which natural habitat they might like to visit. This may require showing them photographs in the books you have provided. Also discuss some items they might include in the Time Capsule. (Possibilities here might include models from a museum exhibition they create, a book written by the company, a documentary video of their journey or the address of a computer web site they design.) Do not worry at this point about the realistic feasibility of their ideas — the agenda here is to strengthen their commitment to believing in the project by allowing them to imagine the possibilities it holds.

Step 5. Responding to the Proposal

The final step your students need to take before they embark on Lesson 1 of this curriculum is to respond to the Sierra Club letter. We suggest that you hold a "company meeting" in which the students dictate to you what they would like to say in their reply. Then you, as the Company Secretary, can draft a final copy of the letter and read it to them for their approval. As you play the role of Secretary, be sure you act only as a helpful advisor rather than as an authority on how the letter should read. Transcribe their thoughts onto paper, raising the standard of their language by making sure it includes proper English and grammar. For example, if a students suggests writing "Yeah, we wanna do it," you would say, as you write, "Our company is pleased to accept your offer." Let them experience the proper language and sentence structure by hearing it as you read rather than by correcting them as they speak. Once their reply has been "sent," you are ready to begin Lesson 1 of *Hooves and Horns, Fins and Feathers: Drama Curriculum for Kindergarten and First Grade.*

NOTE: Although the emphasis of this curriculum is on the development of drama skills, it is also rich in possibilities for learning in other subject areas, particularly the study of animal habitats and behavior. It is highly recommended that you provide learning opportunities related to these topics concurrently with the presentation of this drama curriculum, and that you make resources available to the students in the form of books, videos, pictures, and guest speakers about animals in the wild. A trip to a zoo or wild animal park is also recommended during the presentation of this curriculum.

PART II

PREPARING OBSERVATIONAL SKILLS
FOR *THE JOURNEY*

Now that you have created a dramatic context with your class, you can begin to build your students' drama skills within that context. The following set of lessons focus your students on preparing the observational and recording skills they will need for their imaginary journey into the wild. Students will use their senses to perceive and remember the sights and sounds of nature. They will use their bodies and their minds to accurately recall and recreate what they see. They will practice the skills of nature photography and the making of models to record observations from their journey.

Within the context of preparing for their journey your students will be introduced to some basic tools for drama. They will begin to practice the essential skill of concentration, without which dramatic imagination is not possible. They will engage in activities that increase their body awareness and develop their creative expression through movement. They will explore using their voices to create a mood or setting and will practice working cooperatively with others. As your class begins preparing for their journey into the wild, you will also be providing them with the basic skills they need for a life-long journey into the world of drama.

Lesson 1
Looking and Listening

A. Quiet Listening: *Sounds Around Us*   (5 min.)
B. Move and Freeze: *Photography Practice*   (15 min.)
C. Memory Game: *Name That Animal*   (5 min.)

A. Quiet Listening: *Sounds Around Us*

CONTEXT:
"On our journey we will be using all of our senses to make discoveries about animals. Let's practice using our sense of hearing, as we will need keen ears to hear all of the sounds of the wild."

SKILLS:
Ability to focus attention
Use of the senses

MATERIALS / PREPARATION:
• Clock with second hand, stopwatch, or kitchen timer

PROCEDURE:
1. Make sure students are seated comfortably with their eyes closed. Tell them that they are to stay very still and listen quietly to all the sounds around them for one minute. Challenge them to notice even the quietest sounds.

2. Time the class for one minute. Let them know when the minute has passed.

3. Ask students to name some of the sounds they heard. Examples might be: the clock ticking, people moving, footsteps in the hallway.

4. Repeat the activity once more, challenging students to hear sounds they didn't hear before.

COMMENTARY:

At first, this activity may be difficult for the students as they are not often asked to focus their attention on a single sense. However, with practice, children enjoy this activity greatly and will ask to repeat it again. It is useful for calming a class after outdoor play or at any time you wish to create a mood of focused concentration.

VARIATIONS:

After practicing this activity in the classroom several times, try it outdoors. It is more of a challenge to concentrate when sounds are louder and more numerous, but your students will enjoy trying.

Create a guessing game by asking the students to listen, with their eyes closed, to a sound that you make, then guess what you used to make the sound. Possible sounds might be: pouring water from one container to another, dropping a pencil on the floor, rubbing two stones together, or crumpling paper.

B. Move and Freeze: *Photography Practice*

CONTEXT:
"On our journey we will want to take photographs of the animals we see. Right now we'll practice by taking some imaginary pictures of each other."

SKILLS:
Use of the whole body in movement
Awareness of the body in space

MATERIALS / PREPARATION:
- CD player or tape deck (optional)
- Hand drum

MUSICAL SUGGESTIONS: (optional)
A piece of music with pauses:
   Barlin, Anne, "Freeze and Move," *Hello Toes*
   Chappelle, Eric, "Chirpa, Chirpa," *Music for Creative Dance: Contrast and Continuum, Volume I*
   Palmer, Hap, "Pause," *Movin'*

PROCEDURE:
1. Ask students to find an empty spot in the room to stand, not too close to another person, a wall or piece of furniture. Tell students that when they hear the drumbeats they will walk around the room, being careful not to bump into others. When the drumbeats stop, they will "freeze," stopping immediately and remaining completely still, so you can take their photograph. If your space is very limited, you may have only half of the students move at once with the other half observing, then switch roles.

2. Begin beating the drum, and continue for 15 to 20 seconds. Then stop the drumbeats. As students freeze, pretend that you have a camera and are taking their photographs. As you "photograph" them, comment on the different shapes (body positions) you see,

i.e., "Susan is frozen in a very wide shape. Tommy is frozen in a twisted shape. Jean's frozen shape is low to the ground."

3. Repeat the activity several times, each time encouraging more creative movement choices as the students move to the drum. "Could you move backward to the beat of the drum...sideways...with very large movements...very small movements?" Each time you stop the drumbeats, remind them to freeze in an interesting shape, then take an imaginary photograph.

4. If desired, once the students are comfortable moving to the drumbeats, you may have them repeat the activity to one of the musical suggestions listed above, moving on the musical phrases and freezing when the music pauses.

5. Divide the group in half, having half of the students be movers and half be photographers. This works best if the photographers stand at the edges of the space, allowing the movers to be in the middle. Encourage the photographers to stay alert so they are ready to snap a photo the moment the movers freeze. Have them try photographing from different angles; for example, a student could crouch to get a photograph of a low shape.

6. Repeat the activity, switching roles.

COMMENTARY:
Expressive use of the body is at the foundation of beginning drama experiences. Children at the kindergarten and first-grade levels naturally express themselves and experience the world through movement and will relish doing activities such as the one above. Structured creative movement activities help the child gain a sense of control over his or her body and develop a vocabulary of possible movement choices. You can facilitate this by making verbal suggestions as the students move: *"Have you tried moving in a different direction...on a different level...very quickly...very slowly?"*

VARIATIONS:

To integrate this activity into other areas of your curriculum, ask the students to freeze in specific shapes. For example, they could freeze in the shapes of letters of the alphabet, numerals, or geometric shapes.

To encourage interpersonal interaction, tell students they must freeze in a shape that connects with another person. At first they will probably choose to touch hands as they are connecting. Encourage them to try connecting with other body parts such as heads, elbows, or knees.

C. Memory Game: *Name That Animal*

CONTEXT:
"Nature researchers must be keen observers and be able to remember what they've observed, even at times when they do not have their cameras, sketch pads or other recording devices."

SKILLS:
Ability to focus attention
Use and development of memory

MATERIALS / PREPARATION:
- Create a collage by cutting pictures of animals from magazines and gluing them to a large piece of construction paper or tagboard. The pictures should be large enough for the whole class to see.
- Clock with a second hand, stopwatch, or kitchen timer

PROCEDURE:
1. Hold up the collage and allow students to study it carefully for one minute, with the goal of remembering as many animals as possible that appear in the collage.

2. Put the collage down, then ask the class to name as many animals as they can remember.

3. Hold up the collage again and ask the students to name any animals they missed.

4. Repeat the activity with a second collage, if desired.

COMMENTARY:
This activity provides excellent practice in focusing attention, an essential dramatic skill. The challenge of remembering the animals after the collage has been put down gives students a motivation for shutting out all distracting stimuli for the minute that they are studying the pictures. To further motivate them, let them know exactly

how many animal names they will need to remember. Children will enjoy repeating this activity often.

VARIATIONS:
This activity may also be done using three-dimensional objects on a tray. Try using small plastic animals, available in most toy stores. Doing this activity in a different context, you may also use objects that relate to other areas of your curriculum. For example, if your class is discussing family life create a tray of objects found in the kitchen or objects found in the medicine chest.

As the memory and concentration of your students improves, challenge them further by increasing the number of objects in the collage or on the tray. As an additional challenge, decrease the amount of time they have to study the objects.

Lesson 2
Looking, Listening, and Imagining

A. Quiet Listening: *Sounds of Nature*   (5 min.)
B. Move and Freeze: *Nature Photography*   (15 min.)
C. Mirror Game: *Body Memory*   (5 min.)

A. Quiet Listening: *Sounds of Nature*

CONTEXT:
"Yesterday (or last week, etc.) we practiced using our sense of hearing. Today let's practice again as we create some actual sounds that might be heard in the wild."

SKILLS:
Use of the senses
Expressive use of the voice

MATERIALS / PREPARATION:
• Clock with second hand, stopwatch, or kitchen timer

PROCEDURE:
1. Ask students to name some sounds they might hear in a forest or jungle at night. (Note: If your class is studying a specific natural habitat such as the desert, the rain forest, and so on, you may use that habitat as a focus for this activity.) Examples might include crickets chirping, wind rustling the leaves, owls hooting, lions roaring, monkeys chattering, and do forth.

2. Divide the class in half. Tell half of the students that they will be making the sounds of the jungle (or forest, etc.). Ask each student to decide on at least one sound they will make.

3. Ask the students who will not be making sounds to close their eyes. Tell them they will listen quietly to all the sounds around them for one minute.

4. Start timing a minute, and create a simple narration such as the following: *It is night in the jungle. Very, very quietly the night creatures begin to make their noises...gradually the sounds begin to grow louder...at last they die down as the morning sun begins to rise.* Let the class know when one minute has passed.

5. Ask the listeners to name some of the sounds they heard.

6. Reverse roles and repeat the activity.

COMMENTARY:
In guiding students to begin this activity encourage them to think of sounds that are not immediately obvious such as the sound of animal footsteps, the sound of light rain, the sound of twigs breaking. The greater the variety of sounds they make the richer this experience will be for both the sound-makers and the listeners.

Encourage the sound-makers, through your narration, to begin their sounds softly. This will increase the need for concentration among the listeners. It also serves to provide children who may be self-conscious about using their voices with a less threatening level of participation.

VARIATIONS:
Try making sounds that might be heard in different locales such as the ocean, the city, outer space. Children may have to research to discover some of the different sounds that might be heard in each of these settings.

Read the class a story that takes place in a particular setting, then have them create sound effects to go along with the story.

B. Move and Freeze: *Nature Photography*

CONTEXT:
"Yesterday (or last week) we practiced taking some imaginary photographs of each other. Today we will practice photographing animals in such a way that we won't distract them from their natural behavior."

SKILLS:
Use of the whole body in movement
Use and development of imagination and creativity

MATERIALS / PREPARATION:
- Hand drum
- CD player or tape deck (optional)

MUSICAL SUGGESTIONS: (optional)
A piece of music with pauses:
Barlin, Anne, "Freeze and Move," *Hello Toes*
Chappelle, Eric, "Chirpa, Chirpa," *Music for Creative Dance: Contrast and Continuum, Volume I*
Palmer, Hap "Pause," *Movin'*

PROCEDURE:
1. Repeat the procedure for Move and Freeze in Lesson 1. In this variation, call out the name and movement of an animal (see examples below). When the music or drumbeats stop, students will freeze in shapes as in Lesson 1. When the music or drumbeats resume, call out a new animal name and movement. Encourage students to let their animals move in different directions, on different levels, and to make their movements large or small. Encourage them to try the movements standing rather than being limited to walking on all fours. For the first repetition of this activity all students will move at once, and you will be the photographer taking photographs when they freeze. If space is limited, half of the students may move at once while the other

half observes. Model and point out to the students that you are being unobtrusive as you photograph so that the animals will not be distracted.

2. Repeat the activity with half of the class moving as animals and half being photographers. This works best if the photographers stand at the edges of the space with the animals moving in the center. Remind the photographers to be as quiet as possible as they take their photographs.

3. Reverse roles and repeat the activity once again.

   Examples of animal movements:
   gallop like a pony
   slither like a snake
   jump like a kangaroo
   prowl like a tiger
   scamper like a mouse
   soar like an eagle
   swim like a porpoise
   walk like a bear
   flutter like a butterfly
   leap like a gazelle

COMMENTARY:
As in Lesson 1, continue to emphasize the importance of listening for pauses in the drumbeats or music, and of freezing as quickly as possible so that the photographers will get action shots. Review the idea of making an exciting shape with the body as you freeze rather than simply stopping. This activity is wonderful for developing a sense of body control.

Children love to imitate animals; however, care must be taken that their movement not become stereotypical. Constantly remind them of their many options as they move to encourage them to be creative in their interpretation of each animal. ("Could your pony gallop backward...Could your snake slither on its side or back... Could your bear be huge...Could your bear be a tiny baby?") If playing the drum, use the tempo and volume of the drumbeats to help guide them in varying the size and speed of their movements.

VARIATIONS:

Integrate this activity with your science curriculum by focusing on animals from a particular habitat your class is studying. For example, you might call out the names and movements of desert animals: slithering like a sidewinder, creeping like a tarantula, zooming like a roadrunner; or of undersea creatures: opening and closing like a clam, floating like an octopus, darting like a minnow. You may wish to hold up pictures of the animals as you name them.

Focus on a single movement idea, i.e., animals that move high and animals that move low. Before doing the Move and Freeze activity have the class brainstorm the names and movements of some animals in each category, then use their suggestions as they engage in the activity. Be sure to alternate the two levels for variety. In this case the photographers might want to change their levels as well in order to get the best possible photographs.

C. Mirror Game: *Body Memory*

CONTEXT:
"We will be using not only cameras, notebooks, and sketch pads to record what we observe, but our own memories. We may want to use our bodies to imitate the movements of the animals we see, so that we'll be able to remember them better. Let's practice now by seeing if you can copy exactly what I do."

SKILLS:
Powers of observation and awareness of details
Awareness and control of body parts

MATERIALS / PREPARATION:
• CD player or tape deck (optional)

MUSICAL SUGGESTIONS:
Soft, peaceful music to enhance concentration (optional):
Chappelle, Eric, "Adagio for Two Violins," *Music for Creative Dance: Contrast and Continuum, Volume I*
Palmer, Hap, *Seagulls* (any selection)
Shadowfax, "Dreams of Children," *Dreams of Children*

PROCEDURE:
1. Make sure you are standing in a position in which you can be easily seen by all the students, and that the students have enough space around themselves to move their bodies without touching others.

2. Tell students that their job is to watch you closely and to copy your movements as accurately as possible. Begin to do slow, simple movements with your body, for example: stretching your arms in different directions, nodding or circling your head, shrugging your shoulders, twisting from side to side. Remember to remain facing your students and to stay in one place. The students will move at the same time as you, imagining they are your

mirror images. Continue your movement for one to two minutes, then freeze in a shape.

COMMENTARY:

Mirroring is an excellent beginning exercise in concentration, body awareness, and attention to detail. It is also nonthreatening for students because their attention is on copying you rather than on themselves or each other. You do not need to be an experienced dancer to lead a mirroring exercise; simply think about moving one body part at a time. You will want to keep your movements very slow and simple so they can be easily imitated by the students. Some soothing background music will help alleviate self-consciousness for both you and the children.

VARIATIONS:

As your students build skill in movement, you may want to give volunteers turns to lead the class in mirroring. Make the turns short so the student leaders will feel successful. Children also enjoy doing this activity in partners, with one person being the leader and the other the mirror. Be sure to switch so everyone has a chance to try each role.

You can use mirroring as a regular activity whenever you want to focus the attention of your students. It is a great way to give restless bodies an energy boost after a period of sitting without needing to move furniture or worry about losing control of the class.

Lesson 3
Animal Action

A. Body Part Dance: *Animal Parts*   (10 min.)
B. Sculptor and Clay: *Animal Replicas*   (5 min.)
C. Sculptor and Clay 2: *Replica Museum*   (10 min.)

A. Body Part Dance: *Animal Parts*

CONTEXT:
"Nature researchers must pay attention to detail and be able to notice parts of a living thing as well as the whole. Let's use our own bodies to think about how we might observe some of the body parts of animals."

SKILLS:
Awareness and control of body parts
Powers of observation and awareness of detail

MATERIALS / PREPARATION:
- CD player or tape deck
- Photographs of animals (optional — see Procedure below)

MUSICAL SUGGESTIONS:
Barlin, Anne Leif, "Freeze and Move," *Hello Toes*
Chappelle, Eric, "Chirpa, Chirpa," *Music for Creative Dance: Contrast and Continuum Volume I*
Palmer, Hap, "Pause," *Movin'*

PROCEDURE:
1. Have students find empty spots to stand where they will be able to move without touching others. If space is limited, half of the students may move at once while the other half observes, repeating with reversed roles.

---

2. Explain to students that when you call out a body part such as "head," they are to stay where they are and move only their heads in as many different ways as they can think of. (You may want to demonstrate staying in one place, moving only your head.) When the music stops they will freeze and listen for the next body part to be called.

3. Turn on one of the musical suggestions listed above. (You may also use a selection of your choice without pauses, turning off the music when you want students to freeze.) Call out a body part — head, arms, elbows, legs, knees, hips, fingers, and so forth — at the beginning of each section of music. When the music pauses (or you turn it off), the students will freeze, listening for you to call out the next body part. It will be helpful to call out suggestions as the students move, i.e., "Have you tried nodding your head...Could you move your arms slowly...Could you move both elbows at the same time?"

4. Turn off the music and talk with students about some of the special body parts that animals have, i.e., fins, wings, horns, tails, manes. Showing photographs of animals will be helpful here. Have students discuss which human body parts might correlate or be similarly located to the animal body parts (i.e., arms could be fins or wings, horns and manes would be located on the head, tails would be located on the backside.)

5. Divide the class in half and have half be the movers and half be the observers. The movers will dance the animal body parts you name (don't forget, you can still say "head," "legs," "back," "tummy" and other body parts that are common to both humans and animals, as well). As has been mentioned previously, it is important to call out suggestions as students are moving, such as "Could your fins swim...wiggle...float? Could they move quickly... slowly...smoothly...sharply?" Such questions make the students aware of the many options for movement but are phrased as questions rather than commands. Ask the observers to concentrate on watching the parts that you have named.

6. Switch roles and repeat the activity.

COMMENTARY:
This activity requires a great deal of concentration and use of the imagination as it is only by focusing their attention on the body part you name that the students will succeed in isolating it, and only by imagining themselves to be other than human that they will be able to feel and see their "animal parts." The observers will also be exercising their imaginations as they watch for the movement of fins, wings, and tails.

VARIATIONS:
After students have engaged successfully in this activity several times, they will enjoy playing a body part guessing game. Have several students come to the front of the room (or stand in the center of a circle). Whisper the name of the body part (animal or human) they are to move so only this small group can hear. Turn on music, and have those students move the body part you named. The rest of the class must guess which body part they are showing. Repeat with a new group of students and a new body part.

Enhance your class' study of the human body by calling out more unusual human body parts such as wrist, spine, trunk, heel. These body parts can be a real challenge to isolate in movement.

B. Sculptor and Clay: *Animal Replicas*

CONTEXT:
"There are many ways we may choose to share our discoveries about animals when we return from our trip. We may take photographs and draw pictures. We may also decide to create life-size models of the animals we see."

SKILLS:
Awareness and control of body parts
Development of trust in and empathy for others

MATERIALS / PREPARATION:
- CD player or tape deck (optional)

MUSICAL SUGGESTIONS:
This activity may be presented successfully without music. However, you may find that playing gentle, restful music in the background will increase the care with which students manipulate their partners.

Chappelle, Eric, "Pastarole," *Music for Creative Dance: Contrast and Continuum, Volume II*
Palmer, Hap, "Enter Sunlight" or "Twilight," *Movin'*
Palmer, Hap, *Sea Gulls* (any selection)

PROCEDURE:
1. Divide students into pairs. If there are an odd number of students, ask one student to work with you.

2. Have each pair of students decide who will be the sculptor and who will be the clay. Ask the sculptors to raise their hands so you will know that all pairs have completed this task.

3. The person who is the clay stands still while the sculptor gently moves his or her body parts. The person who is the sculptor must choose an animal, then move their partner's body parts into different positions to create a "statue" of that animal. Once

the sculptor has moved a body part into position the clay must hold it there.

4. When the sculptor feels satisfied with her statue, she must copy it.

5. Students switch roles and repeat the activity.

COMMENTARY:
This activity is a favorite among students and requires a great deal of trust and empathy. It is helpful to demonstrate the activity with you as the sculptor and a child as the clay before the whole class tries it, and to emphasize the need for the sculptors to be gentle as they are manipulating their partner's bodies. The fact that the sculptors must copy their completed statues will help motivate them to put their partners into positions that are comfortable and easy to hold.

You can help enhance the creativity of the sculptors by calling out suggestions as they work, such as "What position will your animal's head be in...its legs...its back? Will it be standing on its hind legs or on all fours? If it is a bird, how will you show its wings? If it is a sea creature, how will you create its fins or tentacles? Will your statue be big or small?"

VARIATIONS:
To reinforce vocabulary in other areas of your curriculum you may ask the students to mold their partners into statues other than animals, i.e., high statues, low statues, straight statues, or curved statues. You may also ask them to create letters of the alphabet, numerals, or geometric shapes.

In the above variations, instead of copying their completed statues you can ask the sculptors to make shapes in relationship to their statues i.e., over it, under it, around it, through it, behind it, beside it, and so on. This is a great way to have the students experience the meaning of prepositions.

C. Sculptor and Clay 2: *Replica Museum*

CONTEXT:
"When we return from our journey we may decide to create an entire museum of animal replicas. Let's see how that might work."

SKILLS:
Awareness and control of body parts
Awareness of the body in space

MATERIALS / PREPARATION:
• CD player or tape deck (optional)

MUSICAL SUGGESTIONS:
See Musical Suggestions for Activity B in this lesson.

PROCEDURE:
1. Divide students into pairs. If there are an odd number of students, ask one student to work with you. (If you are doing this activity immediately after Actvity B, students may continue to work with the same partners, or you may ask them to switch partners for variety.)

2. Have pairs of students designate a sculptor and repeat the procedure in Activity B, with the sculptors molding their partners into a statue of any animal. In this variation, however, the sculptors will leave their partners and stand against a wall of the room when their statues are finished. The statues will hold their positions.

3. When all of the sculptors have finished their models and are standing against the wall, tell them that you are about to open the doors to the Replica Museum. They are to move through the museum and look carefully at each one of the animals. Give them a signal to begin moving through the museum and allow them 1–2 minutes to continue. Give them a signal to return to their partners.

4. Have the sculptor and clay switch roles and repeat the activity.

COMMENTARY:

You may want to conclude this activity by having a discussion with the students about how they feel a museum would work as a way of presenting their research about animals.

The activity also provides an opportunity for a discussion about feelings: How did it feel when your partner was molding your body into a shape? Did you trust your partner to touch you gently? When you were the sculptor, how did it feel to have everyone look at the statue you had created?

VARIATIONS:

You could vary this activity by having the sculptors stop momentarily to copy each replica they see as they move through the museum. This would give them the opportunity to kinesthetically experience some of their classmates' creative ways of molding animal statues.

Instead of focusing on animals, use this activity to enhance learning in other areas of your curriculum. Your students could create a letter museum, a numeral museum, a transportation museum...the possibilities are endless. As your class gains experience in working with others you might ask the sculptors to use two or three people to create a single statue.

Part III

PREPARING SURVIVAL SKILLS AND GEAR FOR *THE JOURNEY*

The journey to observe and record animals will require special skills and equipment. In order to prepare for this journey the group will need to be able to respond quickly, to be resourceful and imaginative with their supplies, and to be able to move silently and stealthily in order to observe the animals. They will need to decide what equipment and other items to pack, and they will need to prepare a map of the territory they will be exploring.

While imaginatively preparing for their journey, the class begins to build skills that are pertinent to all subsequent drama experiences. They develop confidence in making quick responses, "thinking on their feet"; they use their imaginations to create multiple uses for a single object; they learn to control their bodies, movements, and voices; and they expand their thinking to consider all the details required for their drama. At the same time, these preparations help the class to further deepen their belief in their drama so that when they experience the journey itself, their experience will be richer and more satisfying.

Lesson 4
Getting in Shape

A. Quick Response: *Imaginary Balls*   (10 min.)
B. Imagination: *One Object, Many Uses*   (10 min.)
C. Shadowing A Partner: *Silent Shadow*   (10 min.)

A. Quick Response: *Imaginary Balls*

CONTEXT:
"Life in the wild is unpredictable. When we go on our Journey, we must be able to respond quickly and 'think on our feet.'"

SKILLS:
Use and development of imagination and creativity
Use and development of flexible thinking and spontaneity

MATERIALS / PREPARATION:
• Students stand facing you.

PROCEDURE:
1. Explain to students that you will toss an imaginary ball to them, and they must all catch it, then toss it back.

2. Hold an imaginary ball in your hands, clearly showing its size and weight (Is it a basketball? A beach ball? A tennis ball?) Pantomime tossing the ball toward your students.

3. All together, students pantomime catching the ball and tossing it back to you. Encourage students to pantomime the characteristics of the ball as they catch it and toss it back. Repeat several times.

4. Now change the size, weight, or other characteristics of the ball each time you toss it, describing to students what type of ball it

is. Try tossing: a huge ball, a tiny ball, a very heavy ball, a cotton ball, a soft squishy ball, a prickly ball, and so forth. Encourage students to imagine the characteristics of the various balls and to show those characteristics in pantomime each time they catch it and toss it back to you.

COMMENTARY:

This activity provides a beginning experience in the central dramatic concept of using the imagination to create something that is not really there. Creating a single, imaginary object — a ball — provides a foundation for the more complex imaginative experiences to come, when students will be called upon to interact with many imaginary objects and settings, and to believe strongly in premises that they create in their own minds.

Begin this activity slowly, showing students that you see and believe in the properties of the imaginary ball before you toss it. Point out to students that if you toss a big ball it must still be big when they catch it. Practice tossing and catching the original ball several times before changing it.

VARIATIONS:

Focus on descriptive vocabulary by asking students to think of words that could describe a ball. Write the words on a blackboard as you repeat them aloud, then use those words in the activity. Encourage them to think of opposites such as big and small, heavy and light, smooth and prickly. Also encourage them to think divergently by suggesting words that are not usually used to describe balls (i.e., hot, cold, gooey, pointy, and so on).

After doing this activity several times with the class facing you, try standing in a circle and tossing the ball to a student who is next to you, who then tosses it to the next student and so on around the circle. Or, instead of going around the circle, the ball can be tossed in random order, in which case the person tossing the ball first says the name of the person they are going to toss it to. The activity may also be done with pairs of students tossing imaginary balls back and forth to each other.

B. Imagination: *One Object, Many Uses*

CONTEXT:
"When we go on our Journey, we may discover that we don't have everything we need to survive in the wild. We may have to find several uses for each item that we bring."

SKILLS:
Use and development of imagination and creativity
Use and development of flexible thinking and spontaneity

MATERIALS / PREPARATION:
- You will need several familiar objects such as: a hairbrush, a broom, a bowl, and so forth.
- Students are seated in a circle.

PROCEDURE:
1. Show students one of the objects. Ask them to name the object and describe what it is used for. Ask one or two students to come to the center of the circle and demonstrate how that object is normally used.

2. Tell students that you are now going to use that same object in a very different way. Demonstrate using the item in an unusual way. For example: using the hairbrush as a digging stick, the broom as a stirring utensil, or the bowl as a pillow.

3. Ask for volunteers, one at a time, to come to the center of the circle and show another unusual way to use that object.

4. When all ideas for using that object seem to be exhausted (though they never really are!) repeat the procedure with the next object.

COMMENTARY:

This activity encourages divergent thinking and the ability to create an imaginary reality. Although most students will enjoy this activity enormously, it is important at the outset not to pressure anyone to perform before the group. By calling upon volunteers, you allow children to participate at their own pace. As you repeat the activity throughout the year more students will volunteer to demonstrate their ideas.

VARIATIONS:

When you feel that your class is comfortable enough with the activity that most students are willing to participate, pass an object around the circle so that each student in turn can demonstrate a different way to use the object. If anyone does not want a turn, they can pass it on to the next person. See how many rounds of the circle one object can make before your class runs out of ideas!

Use this activity to expose students to a particular culture by employing objects from that culture. For example, if your class was studying China, you could bring in a set of chopsticks, a paper fan, and a bamboo mat. If your class was studying the First People (indigenous culture) of your region, you may be able to get artifacts of historical objects of that culture from your local museum. Have students think of possible uses for each item. Conclude by providing them with information about how the object is or was actually used.

C. Shadowing A Partner: *Silent Shadow*

CONTEXT:
"In order to observe animals in the wild, we must be able to move so quietly and slowly that we will not draw their attention or frighten them. Let's practice following behind a partner, moving slowly and quietly."

SKILLS:
Awareness of body in space
Use and development of powers of observation and awareness of details

MATERIALS / PREPARATION:
- (optional) CD or tape deck
- (optional) tape or CD of quiet, gentle instrumental music

PROCEDURE:
1. As students watch, demonstrate "shadowing": Ask one student to follow behind you while you move, copying your movements as exactly as possible. Move slowly around the room, making simple movements while the student "shadows" you.

2. Divide the students into pairs. Each pair decides (or you designate) who will be the leader (the animal) and who will be the follower (the human). They will switch roles later.

3. You will narrate while the "animals" move and the "humans" copy their movements exactly, without making any sound. Begin by describing the animals asleep, then waking up and going about their business, such as hunting for food:

   "The animals are sleeping. Slowly, they wake up...and begin to go out hunting for something to eat...How does your animal eat its food? Now the animals look for some water to drink." (And so forth.) Keep a slow pace to encourage slow and thoughtful movement. Do not feel that you have to keep up a steady narra-

tive — allow for pauses between your directives. You can play some quiet, gentle music during this activity.

4. Direct the pairs to reverse their roles and repeat the activity.

COMMENTARY:
Shadowing is a basic drama exercise. It requires careful observation and attention to detail. In the context of watching animals, the children relate to the experience of wanting to watch an animal without scaring it away. This activity helps develop control over one's body and movements, which is an essential element of the actor's art.

Begin by narrating the movements of the animals so that the children have a structure to follow and to help them maintain a slow, calm pace. Going slowly requires more self-control than moving swiftly. Your narration provides control over the activity and a focus for the movements. Encourage your students to pay attention to various details of their partner's movements. Which body part(s) are they using? Are their movements sharp or smooth? Quick or slow?

VARIATIONS:
Ask a student volunteer to be the leader while the rest of the class shadows them, following behind in a line, or divide the class into small groups and have one student in each group take a turn as leader. You can also combine shadowing with a Move and Freeze activity by adding a signal to pause and freeze positions, either by beating a drum or by pausing the music.

To continue your study of animals, have the class look at photos and films of animals and observe their bodies and movements closely. What do you notice about how each animal moves? How do they use their various body parts?

Lesson 5
Improvisation

Improvisation: *Zoo Tale*   (20–25 min.)

Improvisation: *Zoo Tale*

CONTEXT:
"To prepare for our trip to see animals in the wild, let's imagine what it's like to be animals in captivity being watched by humans."

SKILLS:
Use and development of imagination and creativity
Expressive use of body and movement

MATERIALS / PREPARATION:
- Whistle or other auditory signal device
- (Optional) Other zookeeper props, such as: a bucket, a hose, and a thermometer — real or cardboard
- Before students arrive, arrange the room with several areas to represent zoo environments and cage areas, such as: Savannah, Rain Forest, Jungle, Ocean, Aviary.
- Make signs designating the zoo entrance and various zoo environments and cages. Using colored paper or cardboard and marking pens, make simple signs with large letters. Add magazine photos or your own drawings of animals found in each zoo area to the signs, to help students decode the words. Hang the signs up so that all students can see them.
- (optional) Signs can also include other ways to name or illustrate your various zoo environments or cage areas. Using such things as pictographs, American Sign Language symbols, or foreign language, you can further challenge students to decode the signs.

PROCEDURE:

1. When students arrive, allow them time to examine and discuss the signs. Simply answer their questions, but refrain from telling them a lot of information unless they ask for it.

2. Ask students to choose an animal they would like to be and to go to where that animal lives in the zoo. For clarity, you can point out each area of the zoo and name the kinds of animals found there.

3. Now you will play the part of the Zookeeper. In this role, you will interact with the animals (students), feeding them, petting them, doing veterinary work, hosing them down with water, and so forth. Meanwhile, you will continually make observations and musings regarding the students' improvised interpretations of animals. For example: *"I wonder why the panther keeps pacing back and forth — I wonder what she's thinking."* Or, *"There is a new baby gorilla born today! Temperature: normal."*

4. Play this improvisation for several minutes. After awhile, resume your role as Teacher and explain to students that you will now add another element to the improvisation:
   - When you blow your whistle (or other signal) all will freeze their positions. While frozen, you will ask them a question, such as: *"What is it like to live in the zoo?"* Or, *"How does it feel when people are watching you?"* Then, one at a time, you will tap a few students on the shoulder, and each will say what they are thinking and feeling as an animal. Questions should be simple and open-ended, not requiring a yes/no response, and should focus on how the animals might think or feel in the zoo environment.
   - On two blows of the whistle, the animals can move again. After a minute or more, repeat the freeze signal, as above.

5. Periodically, you can give a signal for students to become a different animal if they choose. Afterwards, you can have a general

class discussion about the experience and what it felt like. Students may draw pictures or do other art projects from the perspective of being inside zoo cages.

6. End by announcing that the zoo is now closing for the day and all the animals lie down to sleep (the nocturnal animals take a rest as well).

COMMENTARY:

Encourage students to pay attention to the details of their animal's character and to not simply perform stereotyped behavior. For example, if they are being penguins and you see them doing nothing more than just walking around, you can ask them questions, *"How exactly do penguins keep their feathers clean?"* or make suggestive remarks, *"I read somewhere that penguins dive for fish with remarkable speed."*

When the animals speak, refrain from commenting and always take what they say seriously, so that they feel free to express themselves. Even if a student makes a comment that is obviously a joke, you can upgrade the drama by respond earnestly: *"I never knew before that animals have a sense of humor."* In this way, you continue to encourage belief in the improvisation. (Please also see the section "Asking Questions" in Chapter 2, and Chapters 2 and 4 for more about the teacher in role.)

The key to using drama as a learning medium is for students to relate their own experiences and feelings to the subject matter. It's important that you create an opportunity to discover, play, and reflect, rather than turn it into an information-giving session about zoo animals. When students are hooked on a subject, they will seek information, which you can then provide in any number of other, related activities (see below).

VARIATIONS:

Some of the students can volunteer to play visitors to the zoo who then interact with the animals. After awhile, students can choose to switch roles. This sets the scene for an experience of animals in relationship to human visitors, a interaction which will be different from their relationship with the Zookeeper.

You can use the zoo signs to stimulate language arts activities. The zoo signs give students motivation to read the letters or decipher the pictures. As an extension, students can make their own signs for the zoo. This improvisation is also useful for either preparing for or debriefing after an actual field trip to the zoo.

You can provide opportunities for students to explore factual information about animals by setting up a table with books or artifacts. Students can make clay models of animals, or design a map of an animal habitat. For fun, read aloud Dr. Seuss's *If I Ran The Zoo.*

Lesson 6
Visualizing the Journey

A. Sound Story: *African Safari* by Pamela Gerke   (5 min.)
B. Designing and Drawing: *Map for the Journey*   (15–20 min.)

A. Sound Story: *African Safari*

CONTEXT:
"Today I'm going to tell you a story about a group of travelers who went on an African safari. This is a Sound Story, which means you will make the sound effects."

SKILLS:
Expressive use of voice
Use and development of imagination and creativity

MATERIALS / PREPARATION:
- Students will need to be facing you so that they can clearly see the sound signals you will make with your hand and arm. (You can also choose to use an object, such as an arrow, to indicate the signals. Modify the sound signals as needed.)
- Photocopy the following story, "African Safari" to make it easier to hold in one hand while you signal the sounds with your other hand. An alternative method is to write out the sequence of sound cues on the board and tell the story using your own words.

PROCEDURE:
1. Tell students that this will be a Sound Story and go over the rules for the sound signals, below.

   Sound Signals:
   - Make a fist = off
   - Open hand, spread fingers = on
   - Hand raises up toward ceiling = volume increases
   - Hand lowers down toward floor = volume decreases

Have students practice following your signals. Demonstrate all the signals while students make these vocal sounds: 1) birds calling, 2) the sound of wind through trees.

2. Tell the story, using the signals as needed. Feel free to embellish or change the story as you like or make up your own. Pause at the end of each line and make the sound signals while students vocalize the appropriate sounds.

   Generally, begin each sound with the "on" signal at a low volume and slowly increase the volume, allowing students to experiment with making sounds for a few moments. Then slowly decrease the volume to "off" or allow the students to continue the sound, softly, under your voice while you continue the story. Some parts of the story, such as the lion attack, call for an immediate high volume signal.

   If at any time the making of sounds goes beyond your comfort level or becomes too loud for students to hear the next part of the story, simply turn the signal to "off." It's fine if students add gestures as they make sound effects, but they should remain seated.

"African Safari" by Pamela Gerke

This is the story of a group of travelers who went on a safari in Africa to observe the wild animals.

When they first arrive at their camp, the wind is blowing softly through the trees.

Off in the distance they hear birds calling.

The people set up their camp and then go in search of animals. Their boots make soft sounds as they walk across dry grass.

Suddenly, a snake appears!

The snake disappears and the people continue walking. Now they walk through soft, squishy mud.

They come to a lake. Everywhere, there are frogs.

The frogs jump and splash into the water.

Hoping to see animals come to the lake to drink, the people hide behind the bushes and make rustling sounds as they push the leaves aside to make a peephole.

From far away, the people hear the sound of elephants marching. The sound of their pounding feet is faint at first and gets louder and louder as the herd comes closer and closer.

When the elephants arrive at the lake, they noisily suck up water with their big trunks and spray their backs.

The Chief of the Elephants blows her trumpet!

The elephants march away from the lake and the sound of their pounding feet gets softer and softer.

Now a herd of zebras arrives at the lake and stand at the edges of the lake and gently lap the water with their tongues.

Lions attack!

The zebras run away. Now the wind blows, getting stronger and stronger as a storm approaches.

Lightning and thunder!

Rain pours down, fast and thick.

The people huddle under the bushes, shivering so much with cold that their teeth are chattering.

The storm ends and there is silence...

...and then the birds begin to call again.

The frogs croak.

A snake slithers by.

On a distant hill: A lion roars.

The End

COMMENTARY:
Sound Stories encourage expressive use of the voice while actively engaging the imagination with the story. Do not be concerned at first if the students' sounds are tentative or inaccurate. It's best if you do not demonstrate the sounds yourself or tell students how to make them, so that they can make their own discoveries. Use of the sound signals will keep you in control of the activity.

Just as in Move and Freeze activities you employ the dramatic contrast of movement and stillness, here you employ the contrast of sound and silence. These contrasts, as well as light and darkness, are referred to as "the spectra of theater" and can be used in classroom drama to focus attention and to heighten dramatic tension.

VARIATIONS:
Sounds can be made with parts of the body other than voices, such as by clapping hands or pounding the floor. You could also use percussion and other musical instruments. First, decide with the class which instrument will play which sound in the story. For example, maracas can play the sound of the tall grass and the snake, rain sticks can play the sound of rain, drums can play the sound of elephants

and the storm, recorders and kazoos can play the sound of birds and the frogs, and the rest of the sounds can be made vocally.

Sound Stories can also be combined with movement as students mime the actions of the stories while making the appropriate sounds; or, half the group makes the sounds while the other half does the movement (also see Lesson 2A).

B. Designing & Drawing: *Map for the Journey*

CONTEXT:
"We will need a map of the territory we will be exploring on our Journey. Let's decide what the land will look like and draw a map."

SKILLS:
Use and development of imagination and creativity
Collaboration and negotiation with others

MATERIALS / PREPARATION:
- A very large piece of plain paper (or use several large sheets of paper, taped loosely together)
- Tape the paper to the wall at first — later, you will tape it to the floor
- Markers or crayons — enough for all students
- (Optional) Several maps of all kinds can be available for the students to freely examine at any time previous to this lesson.

PROCEDURE:
1. Inform students that together your class will create a map of the territory where your group will travel to photograph animals in the wild. Tell students that you will be drawing the outline of the terrain and that they will then add details and color to the map.

    Explain to students that since your group will be photographing wild animals, you will by necessity be traveling to a natural, undeveloped area and will be camping out when you are there. Ask students for suggestions of the kinds of places in nature where wild animals live and list these places on the board. Your list might include: forest, rain forest, desert, savannah, mountains.

2. Ask students to name the animals that might be found in each place on your list, above. Point out that the type of terrain your class chooses will determine, in part, the kinds of animals you will encounter on the Journey. Together, select the type of territory

your class would like to journey to in order to photograph wild animals. You can make a group decision either by voting or by consensus.

3. Ask students for suggestions about details of your map and where on the map these particular places should be located. As students offer ideas, sketch an outline for each of these details on the map. You will need to decide the following:

   • where your base camp is located
   • where your final designation to observe animals is located
   • the form of transportation needed to travel between your base camp and your final destination (Will you travel in a boat on a river? In a Jeep on a dirt road? By airplane over the mountains? and so forth.)
   • other roadways, waterways (highways, trails, rivers, seas, and so on.)
   • other features of the land as desired (forests, lakes, deserts, mountains,and so forth.)
   • any cities or villages, if desired, and if so, where they are located

   You may want to include a key, such as the symbol for roads, for drinking water sources, animal observation sites, and so on.

4. When students are satisfied with the general outline of the map, divide the class into small groups and assign each an area of the map to detail with drawings and color. Tape the map to the floor. (If your class is too large for all to work comfortably together on the map, you can cut up the areas of the map so that groups can spread out around the room. When the work is completed, tape the pieces back together.)

   While the students are drawing, encourage them to consider the details of the area of the map they are working on. For example, is there a source of drinking water near their base camp? How will they travel from one place to another — do they need to add a roadway or waterway? If a waterway, where will they get the boats needed to travel down the waterway? Students may also want to draw pictures of the animals they would like to see.

If you want the entire map to read right-side-up, draw a compass symbol on the map and explain to students that North points to the top of the paper. (However, spatial orientation is not as crucial here as allowing their imaginations to flow and for students to work well together. It's fine if the map can be read from many angles.)

5. When ready to end the drawing activity for the time being, tape the map to the wall again. (You may need to complete the map at another session.) Add details to the map at any time until the completion of *The Journey* (Lesson 10).

6. Before concluding this activity, ask the class to make two more decisions to help facilitate the Journey:
   • Determine which areas of the classroom will be used to represent various areas of the map, especially Base Camp and the final destination to observe animals.
   • Decide what type of transportation the group will use initially to travel to the land represented by the map and how your group will travel to Base Camp. Will they fly in an airplane? Ride a train? Float down a river?

COMMENTARY:
With the creation of the map you are concretizing the journey and building the students' belief in the drama. Pay attention to all details of their ideas and take their ideas seriously. This is another good opportunity to allow the imaginations of students to flow and for them to make decisions about the creation of their drama. This is also an experience in collaboration, an essential element of theater that develops healthy social skills. You also have the option of having individuals work on map areas alone.

VARIATIONS:

The map could be drawn on the blackboard with colored chalk, as long as the students can reach the top. The disadvantage is that you can't take it with you if your journey takes you to another location. The students could each make their own maps, or create several maps made by small groups. However, in order to experience this journey together as a class, they need to be united in their agreement about the features of the territory they will explore. If you make several, smaller maps, begin by making a list on the blackboard of all the agreed-upon features of the maps.

This activity is a great inroad for studying maps and geography. You can extend it by studying other maps and globes and by visiting a map store.

Lesson 7
Final Preparations

A. Pantomime: *Packing for the Journey*   (10 min.)
B. Improvisation: *At the Passport Office*   (10-15 min.)

A. Pantomime: *Packing for the Journey*

CONTEXT:
"We need to pack for our journey — let's think of all the things we'll want to bring with us. We'll also need to make sure that everything we bring fits into our bags."

SKILLS:
Expressive use of body and movement
Commitment to believing in imaginary situations

MATERIALS / PREPARATION:
• Blackboard and chalk

PROCEDURE:
1. Remind students that they will be camping during their journey to photograph wild animals. Tell students that they will each carry a backpack. Pantomime handing out backpacks, one for each student.

2. Ask the class for ideas of what they will need and want to bring on the Journey. You can have students either call out their ideas spontaneously or raise their hands to be called upon. After listening to each suggestion, repeat the item aloud, giving it your full attention and respect. Have the entire class pantomime picking up and using the object just named and then placing it in their backpack. Ask students for descriptions of the various items they're handling. How large is the item? Is it heavy or light? How do you hold it when it's being used properly?

Continually solicit the students' ideas about what they think is important or essential for the Journey and why.

3. When everything is packed, tell students that on any camping trip, there are many tasks that need to be accomplished. Ask students for suggestions of the kinds of tasks needed in order to keep a base camp running smoothly and write their ideas on the board. Your list might include: collecting firewood, building a campfire, setting up tents, cooking meals, and cleaning up after meals. When you have a list of approximately 4–6 tasks, ask students to sign up for jobs and write their names under each task. Limit the number to 3–6 students per task and make sure every student is assigned a task.

4. At this point, you can go directly to Activity B, "At the Passport Office," where your backpacks will be weighed. If you are not going on to Activity B just yet, pantomime placing all the backpacks in an area of the room, out of the way, and explain to students that they will be retrieving them later.

COMMENTARY:
One of the ways Dorothy Heathcote recommends for internalizing belief in the drama's central imaginary focus (or "The Big Lie") is to engage students in relevant tasks; in this case, deciding what they will need to take on the Journey and packing their backpacks. To heighten the belief in the drama of the Journey, guide your students toward realistically assessing their needs for food, equipment, clothing, and so on. Listen carefully to each suggestion while pointing out the implications of their ideas. For example, if a student suggests bringing along a television in order to watch the weather reports, you might point out that a television would be heavy, cumbersome, and would require electricity that will not be available to you in the wild. When you pantomime handling each item yourself, consider its size, shape, weight, and texture.

VARIATIONS:

This lesson requires students to practice the skill of pantomime. Pantomimes, also called simply "mimes," are a central part of drama education and can be practiced in any number of ways. One possible activity is to choose a subject, such as Animals, Sports, or Household Chores. Students take turns miming for the rest of the class their ideas under the subject heading. For example, if the subject is Sports, a student may choose to pantomime playing baseball or golf. The other students then try to name the sport that is being pantomimed. Students can also do pantomimes in small groups.

Another activity is "Show Me." Ask students to show you pantomimes of various objects, activities, roles, or feelings. For example: *"Show me that you are dialing the telephone. Show me, without making sound, that you are talking to your friend on the telephone. Show me that she tells you something really sad. Now she's telling you a really funny joke."* (And so forth.) Encourage students to be precise in their movements and gestures and to not make any sounds.

B. Improvisation: *At the Passport Office*

CONTEXT:
"Now that our bags are packed, we need to have them weighed. When our luggage passes weight inspection, we can get our passports stamped."

SKILLS:
Understanding and expression of setting
Commitment to believing in imaginary situations

MATERIALS / PREPARATION:
- To prepare their "passports," mark index cards, one per child, with the word *Passport* and the child's first name:

PASSPORT   **(Child's Name)**

- Have ready an ink pad and a rubber stamp suitable for the passport (such as an animal stamp).
- Set up a simple weighing station, for example: a small platform or area rug and a table beside it, on top of which is the stack of passports and the stamp and ink pad. Set up the space so that students will be able to make a single line and go through the station one at a time. If you have another adult assisting, you can have a second station and process the travelers in two lines.
- Also set up a waiting room area with quiet, related activities, such as books, photos, models of animals, and drawing materials.

PROCEDURE:

1. Tell the group that now they must all have their backpacks weighed at the passport office. Pause to briefly discuss passports: what passports are, why travelers must have them, and so on. Explain that in order for the travelers to obtain the proper stamp for their passports, their backpacks must not exceed a certain weight limit. Show students the weighing station and have them line up while they pantomime carrying their backpacks.

2. Tell students that now you will play the role of the Passport Official. As each student comes to the station, you pull out that child's passport and pantomime weighing their backpacks. If you want your students to experience some dramatic tension, you can find that some of the backpacks are too heavy, in which case the student must decide what to leave behind. Or perhaps you can't find someone's passport at first, or don't believe they are who they say they are.

3. After each person's backpack has passed inspection, stamp their passport and, looking them in the eye, say their name and ask them if they are sure they are ready to go on this Journey. When they have responded in the affirmative, ceremoniously give them their passports.

   If a student says "no" to your question or otherwise seems reluctant to participate in the drama, respond to them in your role as Passport Official in a way that insists that they participate in believing in the drama. For example: *"Ah, I see you are giggling. You must be nervous about this journey — anyone in their right mind would be. But what shall it be — are you going or not?"*

   You can also come out of your role as Passport Official and work with the student to establish belief in some part of the drama: *"Earlier, you believed in packing your backpack. Now can you believe in this weighing station?"*

4. After receiving their passports, students pantomime placing their backpacks to one side (from where they will retrieve them when the Journey begins in Lesson 8). They can now go and wait in the waiting room.

5. After all the backpacks have been weighed and passports stamped, collect the passports for safekeeping. You will later put them in the Time Capsule for the children of the future.

COMMENTARY:

This lesson continues the luggage pantomime of the first part of this lesson while adding the element of ritual: the weighing of the travelers' luggage and stamping their passports. Rituals in classroom drama help to build belief and commitment in the drama. Betty Jane Wagner writes of Dorothy Heathcote's use of rituals in order to "…slow the pace and at the same time demand a response of each participant. It constitutes a pressure to reaffirm individual commitment to the drama…Whenever possible, Heathcote employs rituals in which she calls each person by name…The ritual of card-giving upgrades each child's status and helps belief." (Dorothy Heathcote, *Drama as a Learning Medium*)

When you are playing a role in classroom drama, you are not required to be an actor; in fact, Norah Morgan and Juliana Saxton in *Teaching Drama* recommend, "Please *don't* act!" Your job is not to perform or entertain but to convey an attitude that will stimulate imagination and learning, lend a realistic tone to the drama, and provide guidance and information as needed. While taking a part in a drama, your most important role is still that of teacher, continually monitoring the learning experiences of your students and controlling class discipline.

The Passport Official should convey the attitude of authority, a person who has the power to grant permission for the travelers to go on their journey. As mentioned in the Procedure for this activity, the Passport Official can create dramatic tension by being stern and challenging some of the students before reluctantly stamping their passports.

VARIATIONS:

Another adult, such as another teacher or a parent, can be invited to play the role of the Passport Official. Brief your guest beforehand about the kinds of attitudes and behaviors you want them to portray Like you, another adult "in role" should not try to be an actor but rather should project an attitude that will carry your drama forward.

You probably already have rituals in place in your classroom, such as lining up to go to recess, reviewing the calendar together each morning, or giving students awards for good behavior. You can infuse drama into your classroom rituals to add a new dimension and an element of fun. For example, when students go out to recess, they can travel through a "magic" door that will take them to other worlds. When students receive merit awards, you can have each one stand on a box or platform to ceremoniously receive their award while being "filmed by television cameras."

Part IV
ROLE DRAMA *THE JOURNEY*

In the next three lessons you and your students will embark on the most exciting and challenging part of the creative drama experience: the spontaneous role drama. This experience can be especially challenging for the teacher, as it is literally impossible to predict exactly what will happen. But, for this very reason, it also carries a huge amount of potential for learning and growth for everyone involved.

Spontaneous role drama works on a very different model from most educational strategies. Most learning experiences are structured in advance by the teacher, whose plans are then carried out by the students. In spontaneous role drama teacher and students work together to structure an experience at the same time they are engaging in it. Here, the teacher is as much of a participant as the students, and the students have as much control over what will happen as the teacher.

In spite of the apparent risk of such an open-ended activity, the teacher need never fear that she will lose her place as the authority in the classroom. Although the children are involved in decision making in a spontaneous role drama, the teacher always has ultimate control of class management and safety. Following are several guidelines to help you make this spontaneous role drama a successful and fruitful experience for you and your students:

Facilitate Decision Making

Allow your students an opportunity to be involved in appropriate decision making. In initial drama experiences it is best to ask students to choose between a small number of alternatives ("Shall we travel by boat or by train?") rather than giving them an open-ended choice ("How shall we get to our destination?") You can also progressively narrow down choices: After a group has made the choice to travel by land rather than by sea or air, their next choice can be whether to travel by bus or by train.

It is quite common for children to make choices that seem inappropriate ("Let's cut down that tree!"). Your job, as a teacher, is to make them aware of the implications of such choices to their drama rather than to reject their decisions or moralize. For example, when faced with the comment above you might say, "I wonder how many wild creatures live in that tree." In this way you let your students know that their ideas are being heard and considered, but that every idea carries with it a consequence that they must be prepared to accept.

In a role drama some decision making can be done by voting while other decisions are best made by consensus. There will also be situations in which it is fine for you, as teacher, to make a decision yourself in order to keep the momentum of the drama going. See Chapter 4 "Managing Drama Activities in the Classroom," section on Facilitating Group Decision Making for a complete discussion of when it is appropriate to use each of the decision-making processes mentioned above.

Slow the Pace

Remember that your major goal in a spontaneous role drama is to deepen your students' belief in an imaginary situation and to provide them with the opportunity to have an internal connection to the subject matter they are engaged in — not to create an exciting story with a well-constructed plot line. Because of their experiences with stories, TV, and films, your students may very well want to rush to create a climax. Slow them down, hold them back, keep them focused on the physical tasks that need to be done in their imaginary world. When the pace of the drama is slowed, children are more available for feeling and reflection about what they are doing. If an exciting event does end up taking place, it will be much more satisfying if the students have been challenged to make the setting, objects, and situation of the drama real for themselves. The following are some techniques that may be used when you wish to slow the pace:

- Freeze the physical action and ask a reflective question (see the Danger section in *The Journey: An Example* for an illustration of this technique).

- Have the students perform their physical actions in slow motion.

- Restrain the students from moving the story line forward prematurely by asking them to engage fully in a repetitive physical task within the drama, such as collecting wood, sweeping the tent, moving rocks, and so on.

- Delay and build anticipation about the arrival of a character or event by asking the students to form visual images of what it might look like. (See the section Gathering for Breakfast, Foreshadowing the Danger in *The Journey: An Example* for an illustration of this technique.)

Provide Opportunities for Reflection

One of the most important reasons for doing a spontaneous role drama with your students is for the reflection on oneself and one's relationship to the world that such an experience provides. Rather than simply doing a drama, students need a chance to think about what they are experiencing and feeling. We have structured several reflective questions into the outline of *The Journey*. In asking a reflective question you are encouraging, rather than demanding, that students share their thoughts and feelings. Avoid asking questions that begin with the word "why," because such questions may cause students to become defensive, thinking that they are being asked to justify themselves. Asking questions that may simply be answered "yes" or "no" rarely lead to real reflection. The best reflective questions are concrete and relate directly to what the student is experiencing in the drama: "What are you thinking about as the tiger emerges from the cave?" Reflection can also be encouraged through statements of observation about elements of the drama: "I wonder if the tiger senses our presence?" (Also see sections on Asking Questions and Facilitating Reflection in Chapter 2, "The Classroom Teacher as Drama Instructor.")

Structure of *The Journey*

Because of the unpredictable nature of spontaneous role drama, we have provided you with both an outline of the drama with possible alternative courses of action for students to choose from and with a scripted example of how the lesson might progress with a group of kindergarten or first-grade students. Please do not regard the example as a set script to work from or you will deprive your students of the opportunity to make decisions about their own drama.

We have outlined *The Journey* to be completed in three, thirty to forty-five minute periods. You may decide, however, to make it shorter or to extend it over a longer period of time. This is fine; just be sure that you find logical places to break the action so that interest will be sustained. For the sake of continuity, we suggest that you do *The Journey* on consecutive days rather than having a week or several day's break between each session.

Lesson 8
The Journey, Part 1

The Journey, Part 1   (30–45 min.)

The Journey, Part 1

CONTEXT:
"We have been working hard to prepare for our journey into the wild. Today our adventure begins!"

SKILLS:
Commitment to believing in imaginary situations
Story creation / Playwriting

MATERIALS / PREPARATION:
- Post the map of the Journey, created in Lesson 6, where it will be visible to all students.
- Set up chairs, one for each student, in one area of the room to simulate seating on a plane or train. If this is not possible, children may be seated on the floor in a designated area when traveling.
- (Optional) CD player or tape deck
- (Optional) CD or cassette tape of nature sounds, preferably sounds specific to the habitat your group has chosen to visit. Such CDs can be found in New Age supply shops or shops that carry nature-oriented products.

PROCEDURE:
1. **Preparing for Departure.** Give students a choice of traveling to their base camp by train or by plane. (Note: You may decide that other options for transportation will work better for your group, such as traveling by boat or bus. We suggest, however, that you give no more than two alternatives in order to make group decision making easier in this beginning stage.) Ask students to

---

gather their luggage from where they left it in Lesson 7B "at the Passport Office" and line up to "board" their chosen form of transportation. They will need to stow their luggage and fasten their seatbelts. When all are seated, make a reflective statement such as *"We are leaving behind the safety of our homes and venturing into a place where many things may happen. We do not know when we shall return. Is everyone ready to make such a journey?"*

Allow students a moment or two to think about the implications of your statement. You are not necessarily looking for a verbal response to your question, though you may get one. Simply listen openly to any concerns that students may express about leaving their homes or going on the journey. When you feel ready, tell the imaginary pilot or driver of your vehicle to start traveling.

2. **Traveling to Base Camp.** Now your journey has begun! As you sit in the plane or train with your students you might comment on what you are seeing out the window. Ask students to look carefully and silently notice what they are seeing. Tell them that when you touch them on the shoulder they may say aloud what they are seeing through the window. Touch as many students as you wish and allow them to share their visual images.

3. **Setting Up Base Camp.** Tell the pilot or driver to stop, as you have reached the base camp, where you will be spending the night. Ask the students to get off the plane or train and gather their luggage. (Optional: Turn on CD or cassette tape of nature sounds to set the mood of a new environment.) Tell students that they are now responsible for setting up the base camp. Designate three or four tasks that need to be done, for example: gathering firewood, setting up tents, preparing food for dinner, unloading and organizing the photography equipment. Allow students to choose which task they will work at. You might say *"Let me have all the firewood gatherers over here. Your job is to collect bundles of firewood and put them near the fire pit, which is right*

here in the center of our camp." Clearly specify to each group what their task is and where they will do it.

Allow students to work on their tasks for about five minutes, or as long as the activities hold their interest. Challenge them to really feel and see the objects in their environment: to see the twigs they are gathering, to hear the sound of the rushing stream, to feel how hard the ground is when they hammer in the tent stakes, and so forth. Do not let them get away with just pretending to do something — demand that they work as hard at their task as if it were real.

4. **The Campfire.** When base camp has been set up, ask the wood gatherers to build and light the campfire. Ask one of the food preparers to call everyone to dinner. When everyone is seated around the campfire, compliment them on how hard they worked to set up base camp. Let the food preparers describe what they have prepared for dinner as everyone eats.

   After dinner you might suggest some songs around the campfire. Ask the students if they have any songs they would like to sing or suggest one yourself. You may want to toast marshmallows by the campfire.

   As the end of the evening draws near, change the mood of the campfire gathering to a more thoughtful one. Make a statement such as *"You know, this journey we're taking is really risky. Here we are, far away from home, in a place where many dangers might befall us. I wonder what might be some of the dangers we'll face?"*

   Allow students to respond to your question. As you listen to their responses note any that seem to resonate with many of the students. As a group, make a decision about what kind of danger they will be faced with the next day. Decide what will happen, but not when or how. Some possible dangers that could be faced on the Journey include: getting lost, being attacked by wild animals, being attacked by native tribespeople, a fire, and so on. For more information on making this group decision see *The Journey: An Example.* Though it may seem anticlimactic to preplan a dramatic conflict, a sense of anticipation is still present by virtue of the students not knowing exactly how or when the event will take place.

As you will not be able to use every idea that is suggested, you must use your judgment and intuition to steer your class toward the possibility that will best lead them in the direction of becoming deeply involved in their drama. To do this, encourage them to look at the implications of each choice that was suggested.

To give an example of this, imagine that two major dangers were suggested: getting lost in the forest and getting attacked by wild animals. Which of these two possibilities your class ultimately chooses will depend on what they wish to experience. You can point out to them that if they were to get lost they might experience frustration, fear, and a feeling of accomplishment when they get back on track. If they were to be attacked by wild animals, they might feel panic, pain, bravery, and success in getting away (if they are able to). You can guide them in their decision making by asking a question such as *"Would you rather experience the fear of being lost, which starts small but slowly gets stronger, or the fear of a wild animal attack, which happens all of a sudden, without any warning."*

As a teacher, you should be aware of the fact that each of these possibilities also has a different potential implication for what the students will ultimately take away from their drama. The experience of getting lost and then finding their way might give the class a sense of their maturity and of their ability to pull through a difficult situation and persevere in meeting their goals. Being attacked by wild animals might bring them to the conclusion that, although animals are beautiful to watch and important to preserve, they also belong to the world of nature and can be dangerous to humans. Neither of these conclusions is "better" than the other, simply a different choice.

Another element you and your students may want to look at in choosing a dramatic tension is the "chaos factor." It is possible that a wild animal attack might result in a roomful of running, screaming students! If the group chooses an animal attack, help them to plan the attack in such a way that chaos will not be the result. For example, you might tell the students that you want to see four still photographs of the animal attack taking place. With one or two students acting as animals, they would have to plan a sequence of four frozen positions that show the progression of a group being attacked by animals. In this way, they get to experience the fear and excitement of the attack within a structure that provides an element of control.

5. **The Pledge.** Once a decision has been made at the campfire about what danger will present itself the next day, remind the students of their mission: *"We are here to observe and photograph animals in their natural habitat so that future generations of children will know about the beauty of the animals on this earth. We must take a solemn pledge that we will complete what we came here to do, no matter what happens. A pledge is a promise we give to each other. Then, if one of us feels like turning back, the others can remind that person that we are counting on them to keep their promise. We could make the promise one at a time or all together."*

Let students decide how they wish to take the pledge — whether it involves a special handshake, a verbal promise, or some other symbol of commitment. When all have taken the pledge, tell them that it is time to sleep so they will be rested for tomorrow's adventures. Remind them that tomorrow they will see the animals they have come all this way to photograph. Ask the students who set up the tents to quietly lead everyone to their sleeping places. End the lesson with everyone sleeping in their tent.

COMMENTARY:

Doing spontaneous role drama requires an ability to facilitate group decision making. Handling group decisions is discussed both in the Introduction preceding this lesson (Facilitate Decision Making), and in the section on Facilitating Group Decision Making in Chapter 4, "Managing Drama Activities in the Classroom."

As has been mentioned several times during this lesson, you are not always being the teacher during this drama activity, but often a fellow traveler with only slightly more authority than your students. You are still controlling the action to a certain degree, but from inside the drama rather than from outside. This is known as being "in role." In guiding this lesson you will find yourself naturally stepping in and out of role as you participate in the drama, then deal with an organizational or management detail as a teacher. You will find that students accept your dual role quite naturally, and that it will enhance the student-teacher relationship in other areas of your curriculum. (See Chapter 2, "The Classroom Teacher as Drama Instructor" and Chapter 4, "Managing Drama Activities in the Classroom" for more on teacher-in-role.)

Making the pledge at the campfire is an important moment in this drama. In Dorothy Heathcote's work such a moment is known as a "ritual of commitment." It is a time when the students are asked to restate their commitment to believing in the situation they have created. Because it is so crucial to the rest of the Journey, the taking of the pledge should be approached with great solemnity.

VARIATIONS:

Rather than conducting the entire Journey in your classroom you may have the students actually move through the physical space of the school building. Some events in the Journey might take place on the playground, for example, in an empty cafeteria, or auditorium.

You may choose to tape-record the answers to some of the reflective questions for inclusion in a "journal" of the Journey. Or, you may want to invite several parents into the classroom to act as recorders, writing down some of the children's thoughts.

Lesson 9
The Journey, Part 2

The Journey, Part 2   (30–45 min.)

The Journey, Part 2

CONTEXT:
"Today promises to be the most exciting day of our journey, for we will at last complete what we set out to do, no matter what happens."

SKILLS:
Awareness and expression of inner thoughts, feelings, and values
Public presentation: the outward expression of inner thoughts and feelings

MATERIALS / PREPARATION:
- Map (created in Lesson 6) on the wall
- Between the completion of Lesson 8 and the beginning of today's lesson you, as the teacher, will need to plan to create a situation of dramatic tension based on the decision that was made by the group at the campfire about what type of danger they will face. Since the students have decided what will happen but not how or when, it is your job to plan how the event might take place in a way that would most successfully integrate the students' ideas, further your educational goals, and support your effective management of the group and the activity.

You will want to decide, before this lesson begins, how you will foreshadow the dramatic event for the students — will they wake up to find paw prints (cut out of construction paper and placed by you) in the camp? Will there be rips in the map that look as if they were made by giant claws? Will there be a message (written by you) in symbols left by a jungle tribe? Or will there simply be a comment

---

you make or a question you ask that begins to build the dramatic tension for the day? (See Procedure below for suggestions.)

You may also want to decide on any strategy you wish to use for presenting the event. You may want to ask a student to play the role of a wild animal or a person from a local tribe. You may decide to invite a parent or other adult to make a guest appearance "in role" as a ranger or firefighter. You may decide that, for management purposes, the climax scene would be best played out as a series of frozen tableaux (as in the case of a wild animal attack) rather than through realistic action. But be aware that, no matter how carefully you plan, the drama belongs to the students and the ultimate outcome of the dramatic conflict will have to be decided by them.

PROCEDURE:

1. **Gather for Breakfast; Foreshadow the Danger.** Begin where you ended Lesson 8, with everyone (including yourself) asleep in their tents. Tell students that the sun is coming up, and that you will need to get started before it gets too hot. Ask them to pack up their gear and their photography equipment, then meet you at the campfire for breakfast. Allow a few minutes for students to pantomime the above.

   As you are seated at the campfire you will need to do an action or make a statement that will foreshadow the event you have planned. For example, if the group is to get lost you might say, *"Everyone be sure you have your compass with you. I've heard of people getting lost in this jungle and never finding their way out."* Or, if there is to be a wild animal attack you might say *"Hey, everyone, come over and take a look at these paw prints!"* In neither of these examples are you the teacher telling the students what is going to happen: You are speaking in your role as a fellow participant on the journey.

2. **Start Out Toward Your Destination.** You may want to gather students at the map and review where you are going to see the animals and the route you will take to get there. What you do here will depend on how you and your students have decided to

travel: Are you hiking to your destination? Are you riding in a Jeep? Canoeing? Continue to focus students on physical tasks and sensations such as feeling the heat of the day, hearing the sounds of the jungle, pulling the oars of the canoe, looking for animals through their binoculars. Also continue to forecast the upcoming dramatic event: *"Are you sure this is the way?"* *"I thought I heard a lion growl, did you?"*

3. **Accomplishing the Mission.** Now you and your group have reached the habitat of the animals you have come to see and finally have a chance to do what you set out to accomplish. As you approach your destination, you may want to make a reflective statement such as *"I wonder how an animal feels to see humans in its home?"* In general, be aware of any points during the Journey when you can make statements or ask questions to encourage students to reflect on what they are experiencing.

   Ask students to be on the lookout for the first signs of an animal. As their enthusiasm for encountering the animals builds, some children may begin to point out animal tracks or actually begin to "see" the animals themselves. At this point, stop the movement of the group and have everyone begin setting up their camera equipment. Remind students that they need to be very quiet so as not to frighten the animals away. Have each student find a vantage point from which they will photograph the animals. Ask the group to take their pictures in silence. When you tap someone on the shoulder or say their name, that student may describe to everyone the photograph he or she is taking, for example: *"I'm taking a picture of a mother bear and her cubs. They're hiding in a tree."*

4. **Danger!** Now that the group's mission has been accomplished, they are ready to encounter the conflict situation they have chosen. What happens here will depend on what the students have chosen to experience, how you have planned the event, and how the children respond. You may decide, as has been mentioned previously, to use a student or an adult "in role" to facil-

itate the unfolding of the drama (for an example of this, see *The Journey: An Example.*) You might decide to limit the chaos factor by having the conflict scene occur as a series of frozen tableaux. Whatever you decide, be sure to restrain the students from their natural desire to take quick action. Have them tiptoe up to the lions' den and listen for sounds, or have them try several routes before they realize they are actually lost. Be sure there is a sense of resolution to the scene — that they do find their way or escape the danger, even though a few of them may be injured or even killed. Above all, allow the scene to belong to the students — refrain from controlling the outcome or giving them excessive directions as to how things should happen. Be a participant in the scene rather than an observer.

5. **Getting Home.** When the conflict scene has come to a resolution, tell the students it is time to begin the journey home. Let them know that they must hurry, because there is an awards ceremony planned upon their return. Retrace your steps getting back to base camp, and from there back home. The return Journey should be much quicker than the arrival, without as much attention to detail. Your focus here is on the goal of getting home rather than on the details of traveling.

COMMENTARY:

As in *The Journey, Part 1* (Lesson 8), you will often be in role during this lesson as a fellow traveler in the drama. For this lesson you may also want to ask a student to play a special role (see *The Journey: An Example*) or to ask an older student, a parent or other adult to play a role in your drama. When preparing an outsider to play a role, emphasize the importance of neither giving the students too much information nor manipulating the action, but rather letting the children discover who the "in role" character is and why they are there. The purpose of a guest "in role" is to spark the natural curiosity of the students and deepen their involvement in the drama. Therefore, the focus of the guest should be on conveying an attitude that evokes a variety of possible student responses rather than on "acting" or creating a story line.

During the "Danger" portion of this lesson, you may find that one or several of your students are very interested in being killed or dying during the conflict. Though this may cause some discomfort for you, it is important to allow the children to experience this if that is what they choose. As in any point in the role drama of the Journey, the teacher should be willing to go along with any decisions the students make without moralizing so that the drama truly belongs to the students. The teacher, however, can and should point out the implications of the students' decisions without the intention to control the outcome.

You can check your students' commitment to having someone killed during the conflict by reminding them of the implications of this choice: "If you die now, you won't be able to be with us at the awards ceremony." If one or more students do choose to die, you will need to let the rest of the class decide how they wish to handle it. Do they wish to bury the body in the wild? Do they wish to have a funeral when they get home? You may wish to have a stuffed animal or doll stand in for the body so the student can continue being engaged in the drama. Dealing with death in a dramatic context provides children with a safe arena for exploring their concerns, fears, and ideas about this important subject.

VARIATIONS:

If you feel that the danger situation the students have chosen (such as getting lost) will not provide sufficient dramatic tension, you can introduce further tension by creating a limitation of time, space, or resources. For example, if the students have decided that they will get lost, tell them that it will be dark in a few hours or that they will soon run out of food or water.

You can use the structure of this journey to take your students on other adventures such as a journey to the bottom of the ocean, a journey to a foreign country they are learning about, or a journey into outer space.

Lesson 10
The Journey, Part 3

The Journey, Part 3   (30–45 min.)

The Journey, Part 3

CONTEXT:

"We have arrived home from our journey safely and feel proud that we have accomplished our mission. Today we will complete our journey by taking part in an awards ceremony and creating a Time Capsule for the children of the future."

SKILLS:

Recalling and verbalizing about an imaginary experience

Using an imaginary experience to stimulate expression in visual art

MATERIALS / PREPARATION:

- "Award" for each child, which could take the form of:
  - A certificate of completion with the child's name on it.
  - A medal made from cardboard cut into any shape and covered with aluminum foil, with a safety pin to pin it to the child's clothing. The medal could be decorated with the child's name or a symbol scratched into the foil.
  - A ribbon, made from wide, colored ribbon cut into approximately 10 cm. lengths with a safety pin attached to the back. The ribbon could be decorated with the child's name or a symbol using a marker or glitter glue.
- An empty, medium-sized cardboard box. You may want to decorate this box with magazine photographs or student drawings of animals.
- Heavy construction paper or light tagboard cut into 10 x 15 cm rectangles, at least four for each student, laid out on tables along with markers or crayons (see below)
- Markers, crayons or other drawing implements, enough for all students
- Enough space for all students to sit in a large circle

PROCEDURE:

1. **Awards Ceremony.** Ask students to sit in a designated circle for the awards ceremony. You may either play the "Master of Ceremonies," or have another adult such as a parent, another teacher, or administrator come in for a guest appearance as a representative of the Sierra Club. Whoever leads the ceremony should commend the students on their resourcefulness and bravery in completing their mission, and for their generous contribution to children of the future. As you present each child with an award, ask them to share the one thing they will remember most about their Journey. You may want to tape-record their answers or have another adult in the classroom write them down.

2. **Creating a Time Capsule.** Tell the students that they will now be creating a Time Capsule to be opened by children in the future. The Time Capsule will contain any artifacts they create as a result of their Journey. Show them the cardboard box that will contain their artifacts.

   Give each student four of the 10x15 cm rectangles and some drawing implements and ask them to create four or more "photographs" that they took on the Journey. Most of the photographs, of course, should be of the animals they saw, but they also might want to include one of themselves or of one of the events of the Journey. Allow students 15–20 minutes to complete their "photographs." If you have other adults present in the room, ask them to help by labeling the photographs as the students dictate, for example writing "This is the tiger that we caught" below a child's drawing.

   When the students have completed their drawings, ceremoniously take out the cardboard box and ask the students to line up one by one to drop their photographs inside. Let the students know that they will be adding to the box over the next few weeks as they create more artifacts from their Journey. Your Time Capsule can contain any or all of the following:

   • "photographs" created in this lesson

- map created in Lesson 6
- passports
- tape recording or written record of student statements at the awards ceremony
- other items (see Variations below)

COMMENTARY:

This last lesson of the three-part Journey gives students an opportunity to recall their Journey as a past event and to begin to see its implications for the future, thus shifting the perspective of the students from being participants in the experience to being recorders of it. Speaking about their memories and creating photographs are acts that lend significance to what the students have experienced. The making of photographs represents a culmination of the events that began with their commitment to the Sierra Club proposal and therefore should be treated with great respect — this is not just an art project but an opportunity for each child to share what he or she saw and experienced in the imaginary environment.

VARIATIONS:

You can have students create other artifacts to put in the box, such as clay models of the animals they saw. You could also have the students create a book of their Journey to go in the box, with each child contributing a drawing. As with the photographs, you or another adult can write down any words each child wants to say about their picture.

The Journey: An Example

The following is an example of how Lessons 8, 9, and 10, the Journey, might be presented to a kindergarten or first-grade class, along with the students' possible responses. Be aware that this is only one possible outcome of the lesson and is not a script that you or your students must follow.

The Journey, Part 1

1. Preparing for Departure.

As Mr. Jones' students enter the classroom today, they notice that all the chairs have been organized into neat rows along one side of the room. They also notice that the map that they had designed and created last week is hanging on the wall. Curious about these changes, they begin to question Mr. Jones, who assures them that today is the day that they will embark on their Journey.

The class had decided as they made their map that they would be traveling to a rain forest. When asked to vote on whether they should travel by train or by plane, most students agreed that they should go by plane since the rain forest is "so far away." Those who had voted to take the train were willing to go with the majority. All of the children eagerly go to the area in the classroom where they had previously stored their imaginary luggage (after visiting the Passport Office), then line up with their luggage next to the chairs. Mr. Jones plays an airline steward who helps each child stow their luggage and find a seat.

When each child has found their seat on the "plane," Mr. Jones becomes a fellow traveler and fastens his seat belt, which he encourages everyone to do. As they prepare for takeoff, he says quietly, "We are leaving behind the safety of our homes and venturing into a place where many things can happen. We do not know when we shall return. Is everyone ready to make such a journey?" After thinking for a moment most of the children reply that they are, and the plane takes off.

2. Traveling to Base Camp.

The students sit in their seats in relative silence, not knowing what is expected of them. After a few moments Mr. Jones leans to look out his window and comments "Look at those fluffy clouds out there!" The students are quick to get the idea. "Hey, I see some mountains!" exclaims Elizabeth. Mr. Jones asks everyone to look out the window very carefully and notice the scenery that the plane is flying over. "Look out your window without saying a word. When I tap you on the shoulder, I'd like you to tell all of us about something you are seeing."

Mr. Jones gets out of his seat and begins walking through the aisles of the plane, searching for students who are concentrating on looking out the window. When he taps Robert on the shoulder, Robert softly says, "I see cars that look as small as ants." "Wonderful, Robert," smiles Mr. Jones. "Could you say it just a little louder so everyone on the plane can hear you?" Robert repeats his statement. Mr. Jones taps several more students on the shoulder and allows them to share their visual images.

3. Setting up Base Camp.

After a few minutes Mr. Jones says, "We're coming in for a landing. We've now reached the base camp where we'll be spending the night before we venture further into the rain forest. Please gather your luggage and get off the plane."

The students follow Mr. Jones to an area of the classroom that has been cleared for the drama lesson. "This is our base camp," explains Mr. Jones. "There are many jobs to be done to set up our camp for the evening. I will need people to gather wood for our campfire, some people to set up the tents, a few to prepare our dinner, and two or three to organize our photography equipment. Think for a moment about which of these jobs you would like to do."

Mr. Jones allows the students a few moments to make decisions. "Let me have everyone who will gather firewood over here. Those who are going to set up the tents please stand there. All those who would like to prepare dinner stand beside me."

The largest group are the firewood gatherers. Mr. Jones points to a corner of the classroom and tells the group that there are some fallen trees that can be chopped up for firewood. He hands them three imaginary axes and tells the group that they must share the equipment. He then points out the imaginary fire pit where they will deposit any wood they gather.

In a similar fashion he directs the tent setters, the food preparers and the equipment organizers as to where and how their tasks will be done. As the children begin their tasks he circulates among them, commenting on and asking questions about what he sees: "I can tell that your ax is very heavy, Sarah! Where do you think would be the best spot for this tent? Mmmm...that smells delicious. What have you decided to make for dinner?" When a boy from the firewood group runs to Mr. Jones and tells him that the group has finished their task he says, "Let me see...no, I believe we will need more wood than that to last us through this night. It takes quite a while to gather enough firewood to last a whole evening."

Suddenly Mr. Jones notices a skirmish breaking out among the firewood gatherers. The other students drop what they are doing and come over to watch. Mr. Jones senses that the group needs to refocus their energy, so he turns off the light switch for a moment, saying "A dark storm cloud is passing over the sun. We'd better make sure our equipment is covered in case it rains this evening." In doing this Mr. Jones is using the contrast between light and darkness to focus attention and heighten dramatic effect.

4. The Campfire.

After the students have once again become involved in the drama and Mr. Jones feels satisfied that the students are beginning to really perceive their imaginary environment and the objects in it through their physical tasks, he asks everyone to gather around to watch the fire being lit. He chooses two volunteers from the wood gathering group to build and start the fire. He does not direct them as to how fires are built; he allows them to be the experts. When the children are satisfied that they are sitting before a roaring blaze, he asks the food preparers to serve dinner. They proudly hand an imaginary plate of food to each child, telling them it is stew.

When everyone has finished dinner Mr. Jones comments that it is getting dark, and stars are beginning to come out. He asks if anyone would like to sing a song. John suggests "Michael, Row Your Boat Ashore," which they all sing.

Mr. Jones asks the students to sit in silence for a moment and listen to the crackling of the fire. After a few moments he says quietly, "You know, this journey we're taking is really risky. Here we are, far away from home, in a place where many dangers might befall us. I wonder what are some of the dangers we might face?"

"Maybe there will be a huge storm," says Elizabeth in a worried voice. "What would be the most frightening part about a storm?" asks Mr. Jones, wanting her to flesh out her idea further. "The thunder and lightning," Elizabeth emphatically replies. "Or we might get lost," suggests Tom.

Robert can hardly contain his excitement. "Maybe we'll be attacked by a wild animal!" he cries. "And what kind of wild animal do you think we might meet in this rain forest?" Mr. Jones asks. "A tiger!" shouts Robert excitedly. "With big teeth and claws and stripes!"

"There are not many tigers left, but there might be some in this rain forest" agrees Mr. Jones. "Now, we have a choice to make:

Would you rather encounter a storm, get lost, or experience a tiger attack tomorrow? A storm might stop us from taking our photographs. If we get lost, it's possible that we might not find our way back. A tiger attack could result in some of us being hurt. Think for a minute about which risk you're most willing to take, then let's take a vote."

The students vote and the majority of them decide they would like to experience the tiger attack. "How do we want the attack to turn out? Mr. Jones asks. "I want to kill that tiger!" replies Robert. "No, I think we should capture it and take it home with us," Sarah suggests. "Yes! Let's capture the tiger!" shout the students enthusiastically.

"Let me make sure I understand what you want," Mr. Jones summarizes. "Tomorrow you'd like to experience a tiger attack, and you'd like to capture the tiger." Most of the students agree on this course of action.

5. The Pledge.

"Well, of course we don't know exactly how tomorrow will go," Mr. Jones comments. "But I think it's important to remember why we came here in the first place. Could someone please refresh our memories about the mission of this journey?"

"We came to take pictures of animals," states John proudly.

"That's right," says Mr. Jones, "We are here to observe and photograph animals in their natural habitat so that future generations of children will know about the beauty of animals on this earth. I suggest that we take a solemn pledge that we will complete what we came here to do, no matter what happens. A pledge is a promise we give to each other. Then, if one of us feels like turning back, the others can remind that person that we are counting on them to keep their promise. We could make the promise one at a time, or all together."

"We should all put our hands together,'" suggests Elizabeth.
The students stretch their hands out to touch each other across the dying embers of the fire to make their pledge. Mr. Jones says "Repeat after me: We the photographers...of ____ (company name)...do solemnly pledge....to complete our journey's mission...no matter what dangers may befall us."

There is a moment of silence before Mr. Jones comments, "The fire is dying out; it must be getting late. I suggest that we all crawl into our tents and sleep, since we have quite a day ahead of us tomorrow. Would the tent group please show us where we are to sleep?"

The eight children who had set up the tents earlier lead the rest of the class to the tent area, showing each child his or her special sleeping place. After a few snores and giggles, it is quiet.

"We'll stop our drama Journey now for today. Let's remember where our sleeping place is so we can go back to it when we continue our Journey tomorrow," says Mr. Jones, once again in his role as teacher.

The Journey, Part 2

After school on the first day of the Journey Mr. Jones spent some time preparing for the following day. He created a certificate of completion for each child in the class. He also put some thought into the decision that the children had made around the campfire, for he knew it would be crucial to add some dramatic tension to the second half of the Journey.

Mr. Jones decided that he could begin the tension by having the group discover a tiger's paw prints in the camp. Using a book on animal tracks as his guide, he cut several paw prints out of brown construction paper.

Mr. Jones further prepared for the lesson by choosing one child, Annie (who had been resisting becoming involved in the drama), to be the one who is attacked by the tiger. During recess on the second day of the Journey, he took Annie aside and told her about the part she would be playing in the day's adventures. Mr. Jones was careful not to tell Annie exactly what to do or how the adventure would go, only that when he whispered in her ear she was to lie down on the floor and pretend she had been injured by the tiger. Also during recess, he placed the construction paper paw prints on the floor in the area where the drama would take place and put several rips in the wall map, making them look as if they were made by claws.

1. Gather for Breakfast, Foreshadow the Dramatic Event.

When the students entered the room after recess, they again saw it set up for their journey. Mr. Jones told them to lie in their tents just as they had when they left off the day before. When everyone was settled and had been lying still for a few moments, Mr. Jones sat up and stretched, then started to walk among the students, shaking them gently. "Wake up, wake up! I have something to show you!"

When all the children had gathered around, Mr. Jones called their attention to the paw prints on the ground. "I found these when I woke up this morning." "It's the tiger!" shouted Robert. "It must have been here last night!" "Those aren't real," said Seth disdainfully. "I can tell Mr. Jones made them out of paper." "You're right, I did make them, Seth. But, just for now, could we agree to believe that they're real?" "I guess," said Seth doubtfully.

Sensing his reluctance, Mr. Jones says, "Just for a moment, let's all stand and look at these paw prints. See if you can imagine that they're imprinted in the dirt." He paused for a moment to let the image sink in. "Now see if you can imagine the tiger that made those prints. What does it look like?"

"It's big," breathed Elizabeth. "It's orange with black stripes." "It's got huge, sharp teeth." "And claws." Mr. Jones allows them to stand in silence with the visual picture they have created. "Hey, look at these rips on the map!" Sarah called out. "Maybe the tiger did that, too."

"Yes, it looks as if the tiger is in the area today — we'd better be extra careful and stick close together," cautions Mr. Jones. "Well, time to get going — we have a long journey ahead of us. Take a minute to pack up your gear and photography equipment and we'll be on our way."

2. Starting Out Toward Your Destination.

When the students have packed, Mr. Jones gathers them at the map. He points out where they are, and the route they must take to get to the animals. The class had already decided that they would be hiking into the rain forest.

Walking single file with Mr. Jones and Tom in the lead, the children walk around the classroom. As they walk, Mr. Jones keeps them focused on their imaginary physical surroundings by making comments and asking questions such as, "It's so hot my shirt is already sticking to me. We'd better stop to have some water." "Listen! What kind of sounds do you hear in the rain forest?" "Would anyone like to stop and scout for animals with their binoculars?"

3. Accomplishing the Mission.

As they get closer to their destination more and more students are reporting animal sightings. "I wonder how an animal feels to see humans in its home," muses Mr. Jones.

"I bet they're scared of us," says Tom. "Or maybe they just think we're interesting, like we think they are," Sarah comments.

"I think we're here!" announces Mr. Jones. "Let's get ready to photograph some animals! Everyone please get your camera ready and go to a place where you can take pictures. Remember, we have to be really quiet so we won't frighten the animals." The students pantomime getting out their cameras and beginning to take photographs. Everyone is so engaged that no one notices Annie slip away to take her place lying on the ground, a few feet away from where the others are photographing.

"Please take your photographs in silence," Mr. Jones says. "When I come up and tap you on the shoulder, you may tell everyone what kind of animal you are photographing, and what the animal is doing."

"I'm taking a picture of a monkey. It's swinging in the trees."

"My picture is of a toucan sitting on a branch."

"I'm taking a picture of a huge snake!"

Mr. Jones gives every student who wishes a chance to speak.

4. Danger!

Once the group has completed their photography session, Mr. Jones tells them to pack up for the hike back to base camp. He does not draw attention to Annie, who is lying on the ground, but rather allows the students to discover her for themselves. Tom is the first to notice her.

"Hey, look!" he cried. "What's wrong with Annie!" Annie giggles a little, but Mr. Jones reminds her that if they want to do the scene about the tiger she must help them believe that she has been hurt. "The tiger got me," Annie mumbles. "It scratched me with its claws."

"What shall we do?" Mr. Jones asks. "Let's hunt for the tiger and capture it!" says Sarah. "But what about Annie?" Mr. Jones reminds them. "Can we just leave her like this?" Robert steps forward confidently and says, "I'm a doctor. I'll fix her."

"O.K. You fix her, and we'll go on ahead to look for the tiger. Join us when you're ready." Then, turning to the others, Mr. Jones asks, "Where do you think that tiger might be?" "Hiding in the bushes over there!" shouts Tom. "No, I think it's in a cave," argues Sarah.

"Bushes or cave, which shall it be? " asks Mr. Jones. "I think bushes because then we can see it easier," Tom answers.

Although Mr. Jones knows that tigers do not characteristically live in caves, he knows that at this moment allowing the students to create the situation as they wish it to be is more important than being factually accurate. "Tell you what," says Mr. Jones, thinking on his feet. "Let's send Tom to scout in the bushes and Sarah to look in the cave. If either of you sees any sign of the tiger, come back and tell us."

Mr. Jones points out the locations of the cave and the bushes clearly, and the students watch anxiously as Tom and Sarah move in their chosen directions. Suddenly Sarah screams and runs back to the group.

"I heard it growl inside the cave!" she cries.

Several students begin to scream and run so Mr. Jones, as their teacher, gives them the class signal for quiet — a special hand-clapping pattern that the children echo.

"If we are going to do this we must really think about what we are doing, and make sure we believe every moment of it. Sarah has heard the tiger in the cave. Let's think about how we are going to capture the tiger."

The students, somewhat calmed, discuss this problem and decide to put a rope around the tiger's neck when it comes out. At this point Annie and Robert join them, and they all organize themselves with the imaginary rope at the entrance of the cave. Mr. Jones decides that, rather than having one of the students pretend to be the tiger, he will encourage the class to see and believe in an imaginary tiger. To do this, he slows the pace of the drama:

"Everyone freeze. The tiger is now coming out of the cave. Don't move or say a word. Just see how big that tiger is. Look at how it walks, how it turns its head and looks at us. Stay frozen right where you are. In a moment I will let you capture the tiger. But first I want to know what you're thinking as you see the tiger coming out of the cave. When I touch you, tell me what you see and what you are thinking."

"It's so big. I'm scared." "It's eyes are looking right at me. I wish I could hide." "It looks like it wants to kill me. I want to go home."

"Now, capture that tiger like you're in a slow-motion movie. Get that rope around its neck. Feel how strong it is and how it's trying to get away."

Mr. Jones guides the students, through his narration, to experience the act of capturing the tiger.

"Now that we've captured this tiger, what are we going to do with it?" he questions the students. "Let's kill it!" shouts Robert. "No, I want to take it home with us," says Sarah. "I think we should let it go," argues Tom. "It only attacked us because we were in its home."

"So," says Mr. Jones thoughtfully, "we can choose to kill this tiger. We must remember, though, that it may be an endangered species, and we might end up killing one of the last of this species of tiger. We can also choose to take it home with us. That might be illegal — we'd have to find out about the laws concerning taking a wild animal from its habitat. We'd also have to figure out how to get it onto the plane, and where to keep it once we got back to our country. I'm wondering if a wild tiger would be happy living in captivity. Our last choice is to let the tiger go free. What do you choose to do with the tiger?"

"If we let it go free," says Elizabeth in frustration, "We will have captured it for nothing!"

"But I'll feel sad if we kill the tiger," Tom comments softly. "I know I'd feel better without the death of a tiger on my conscience," Mr. Jones agrees.

Mr. Jones allows the students to discuss this question heatedly for several minutes. When he asks for a show of hands for each choice, the decision is clearly to let the tiger go. Mr. Jones asks if anyone has any last words to say to the tiger before they release it.

"Thank you for letting us see you, tiger," says Tom solemnly. "We forgive you for hurting our friend, because we know you were just mad because we were in your rain forest."

"On the count of three, let's let go of the rope and wave good-bye to the tiger," Mr. Jones directs. "One...two...three..." The children watch the imaginary tiger slink back into the rain forest.

5. Getting Home.

Now that the incident with the tiger seems to be resolved, Mr. Jones tells the students that they must hurry home, because there is an awards ceremony planned for their return. They hike back to base camp the way they came, then quickly pack up their gear and reboard the waiting plane. When they get off the plane, Mr. Jones welcomes them back to the classroom, and tells them that their drama Journey is finished for today but will continue tomorrow with an Awards Ceremony.

The Journey, Part 3

1. Awards Ceremony.

The next day after recess, Mr. Jones tells the students to sit on the rug at the back of the room. They discover Mrs. Fuller, Elizabeth's mother, waiting for them wearing a badge that says "Sierra Club."

"Young friends," she intones, "you are to be commended for your bravery in accomplishing this dangerous mission. Through you, the children of the future will know all about the wonderful animals that now inhabit the earth. On behalf of the Sierra Club, I would like to present each of you with an award. When I call your name, please step forward and tell me the one thing you will always remember about your Journey."

She calls each child by name, according to the list Mr. Jones has given her. As each child steps up to receive his or her certificate, Mr. Jones writes down their comment about the Journey. Their comments include the following:

"I'll always remember singing at the campfire." "I'll always remember how we let the tiger go." "I'll always remember how happy I felt when we finally saw the animals." "I'll always remember being scared, but being brave at the same time." "I'll always remember how good it felt to do what I promised I would do."

2. Creating a Time Capsule.

After each child has received their reward, Mr. Jones comes forward carrying a cardboard box decorated with pictures of animals cut from magazines.

"Now that we have successfully completed our mission we will create a Time Capsule to be opened by children in the future. The Time Capsule will contain any artifacts we create as a result of our

Journey. We'll put the artifacts in this box, then leave it for the children of the future."

"The first thing we need to put in the Time Capsule are the photographs we took on our Journey. Please take a seat at one of the tables, and draw four or more pictures that show some of the photographs you took. Most of them should be of animals, of course, but you might put in one or two of yourself or some of your friends, showing something that happened to us on the Journey."

As the students draw pictures on the rectangles of tagboard at the tables, Mr. Jones and Mrs. Fuller circulate among them with pens, taking dictation from individual children to label their photographs. Some of the children's labels read: "This is a picture of a parrot in the rain forest." "These are some monkeys playing," "We are singing at the campfire." "This is me catching the tiger." "This is the tiger going free."

When the students are finished making their photographs, Mr. Jones asks them to hold their pictures and form a line. Each child takes a turn to ceremoniously put their photographs in the box. Mr. Jones takes the ripped map from the wall, folds it, and lays it on top of the photographs. Last of all he puts in the children's passports, and his written record of what each child said at the Awards Ceremony.

"We have begun making our Time Capsule today, but we will continue to add to it as we create more artifacts from our Journey."

The End

Part V

INTERPRETING, RECORDING, AND PRESENTING *THE JOURNEY*

In Part V students use several dramatic forms to explore, interpret, and record their Journey experience and to share the experience with others. They recreate the Journey through depiction (*Slide Show*); further explore the animals theme by creating original poetry and movement (*Animal Cinquain*); and analyze, reflect, and communicate their thoughts and feelings about the Journey through public speaking (*TV Interview*).

In these lessons students have the opportunity to observe the effect of their words and actions on others by presenting their ideas to their classmates. The section Public Sharing Event gives suggestions on how to present some of the drama forms the students have created in Part IV to an outside audience — perhaps to another class or to their parents. Students will enjoy the chance to show off, while you, the teacher, will appreciate the experience as one where students monitor the effectiveness of their communication skills and of the symbols they've created (in language, movement, and story) to explicate their ideas. The public presentation suggested here is intended to be informal and enjoyable, with the focus being on a positive experience for your students in "making their private thoughts public."

Lesson 11
Move and Freeze: *Slide Show*

Move and Freeze: *Slide Show* (15–20 min.)

Thanks to Dr. Barbara McKean for the suggestion of "snap and click" and to Kathleen Edwards for the "slide show" idea.

Move and Freeze: *Slide Show*

CONTEXT:
"We've completed our Journey and now we'll put together a living slide show of our adventures."

SKILLS:
Expressive use of body
Ability to sequence time and events
Development of discriminating perception as an audience member

MATERIALS / PREPARATION:
- Before students arrive, make a list of three events or scenes from the beginning, middle, and end of your class' Journey experience. The following is a sample list of events from *The Journey: An Example* in Part IV. Write your list on the blackboard. (Your own list may look quite different.)
  1. Packing
  2. Campfire pledge
  3. Letting the tiger go

- An auditory signal, described as a finger snap in this lesson; however, you can substitute a bell, drum, or other signal
- Space for half the class to depict the slide show, with room for the other half to sit and watch
- (optional) As an additional preparation for this lesson (on the same day or earlier), you can show the class a slide show of any kind (see Variations, following).

PROCEDURE:

1. Briefly discuss slide shows with students. They should understand that slides are another way to show photos, that they are projected on a big screen or wall, and that they are arranged in some sort of order. Explain that in this activity the class will create a living slide show in which the students themselves portray photographs of three scenes from their Journey.

2. Divide the class in half — half will depict the slides first while the other half watches, then they will switch roles. Ask the "slide" students to spread out in the room to create the first slide. Tell them the name of the slide — "Packing" — and spend a few moments working with them to form the pose. For example: Should students be standing or sitting? What actions were they doing when the picture was taken? Should everyone in the group be doing the same action or separate actions? Were they holding any objects? Were they feeling happy, sad, excited, scared? Encourage students to recreate the scene from their memories of it and help them to make accurate poses and facial expressions.

3. When you have a satisfactory picture of the scene, ask students to hold their poses for a few seconds. Tell them to try to remember exactly how and where they are positioned for this slide, as you will ask them to recreate it later.

4. Repeat the procedure with the other two slides on your list.

5. You will now go through the entire sequence of the slide show, this time moving more quickly from one slide to the next as students recreate their poses for each scene. Explain the procedure for "Snap and Click" like this:
   • You will announce the number and name of the next slide (going in order) and students will move to their positions for that picture. For example, "Slide #1: Packing."

- When everyone is in place, you will say: "Click!" and everyone freezes. Students hold their poses for a few seconds.
- You will snap your fingers and students will unfreeze and move to their positions for the next slide.
- You will announce the number and name of the next slide and repeat the procedure.

6. Do the entire slide show with the first group of students. While students are frozen in position, ask the students who are watching to examine details of each scene. For example, "See if you can tell which objects are being packed in the bags." Or, "Notice the expressions on the faces of the travelers when they watch the tiger go free."

7. Switch roles and repeat steps 2–5 with the other half of the class.

8. Copy your list of slides onto paper for future use and to be placed in the Time Capsule.

COMMENTARY:

Depiction, also called tableaux or freeze frame, is a form of "concretized thought." In looking at your students' slides, you may be able to evaluate your students' impressions and ideas with regard to their Journey experience. This activity also involves working with a simple dramatic form: a sequence with a beginning, middle, and end.

In this lesson the teacher encourages students to pay attention to details of bodily gesture and facial expression. By showing the slides to an audience — in this case, their classmates — students are making public their ideas about the Journey experience and seeing the effect of their actions on others. The emphasis here is not on performing but on sharing ideas and impressions and on evaluating how effectively one's own expressions communicate to others. You can reduce the pressure of being watched by keeping the slide show simple and making sure the rules of "Snap and Click" are clear.

Sharing with others can be a pleasurable learning experience if there is no pressure on students to perform. Direct the attention of your students (both audience members and presenters) to details of each slide, encouraging them to use their powers of observation. You can "...(make) the 'showing' part of the learning experience, so that it is seen as an element of the process, not the result...looking at other peoples' work will enable them to compare, pick up an idea or two and perhaps discover a new perspective which will deepen the meaning for them." (Norah Morgan and Juliana Saxton, *Teaching Drama*)

With any experience of sharing/showing in this curriculum, students learn about how to be good audience members with regard to proper etiquette and intelligent observation. When you teach audience members to be discriminating viewers, you also help the presenters pay attention to details of their expression. You can allow audience members to make comments about what they see as long as their feedback is specific to the content of the slides and does not contain hurtful criticism.

VARIATIONS:
Before doing this lesson, you might like to present a slide show to your class to give them a better understanding of slide shows and to remind them of the viewer's perspective.

You can extend the lesson by soliciting ideas from your students for additional slides for your slide show. For a lesson on sequencing events: change the order of the slides and ask students which sequence they prefer and why. Or, give each student the pictures they drew in Lesson 10 and ask them to put them in some sort of order. Then you, or the student, can number each picture in order. This will encourage numeral recognition: After their pictures are assigned numbers, shuffle them and have students put them back in order.

Lesson 12
Poetry in Motion

Poetry in Motion: *Animal Cinquain* (20 min.)

Poetry in Motion: *Animal Cinquain*

CONTEXT:

"Another way for us to present our animal observations to the Sierra Club is by doing movement to poems about animals."

SKILLS:

Expressive use of body and movement
Artistic collaboration

MATERIALS / PREPARATION:

- Blackboard and chalk
- CD player or tape deck (optional)
- The following cinquain (five-line poems) written on the board:

> Tigers
> Strong, fierce
> Waking, prowling, attacking
> Feeding on their kill
> Tigers

> Monkeys
> Small, active
> —————, —————, —————
> Swinging from tree to tree
> Monkeys

OPTIONAL: Instead of poems about tigers and monkeys, you may choose to present poetry about other animals. Write your poems in the following form:

Noun (name of animal)
Adjective, Adjective (two words describing the animal)
Verb, Verb, Verb (three actions done by that animal, each ending in "ing")
Phrase (a phrase about the animal)
Noun (repeat name of animal)

MUSICAL SUGGESTIONS:

For the tiger poem, a strong powerful selection such as:
Greig, Edward, "In the Hall of the Mountain King," *Peer Gynt*

For the monkey poem, a playful selection such as:
Palmer, Hap, "Changes," *Getting to Know Myself*

For poems about other animals, choose musical selections that evoke that animal for you. You may also present this activity without music.

PROCEDURE:

1. Read the tiger cinquain aloud to the students.

2. Go through the poem word by word, discussing how each word or phrase could be put into action. Solicit ideas from the students as to how they think the group should move during each part of the poem. Model collaboration by negotiating with students about which of the proposed ideas to use, or how several ideas could be put together. You may want to write notes about the group's decisions next to the appropriate word or line in the poem to aid memory. Example:

Tigers (*A group of students, acting as tigers, walk on all fours to the center of the space.*)
Strong (*The tigers pose.*)
Fierce (*The tigers roar.*)
Waking (*The tigers wake up.*)

Prowling *(The tigers prowl while a group of students playing smaller animals walk by.)*
Attacking *(Each tiger chases and catches an animal.)*
Feeding on their kill *(The tigers mime eating the animals.)*
Tigers *(The tigers pose together.)*

3. Have the students perform the poem as planned while you read it aloud. You may have the whole class move at once, or in smaller groups with the remainder of the class being the audience (see Commentary, below).

4. Read the monkey poem aloud. Ask the students to help you fill in the blanks with three words ending in *ing* that describe the behavior of monkeys. Write the words they choose in the blanks to complete the poem.

5. Repeat steps 2 and 3, having students plan and then perform actions to go with the poem.

6. Repeat with poems about other animals, as desired.

7. Later, write all poems you have worked with on paper and add them to the Time Capsule.

COMMENTARY:

Most children find moving to poetry highly satisfying because it sparks their natural sense of rhythm and musicality. The cinquain is a good form to start with because it is short and concrete, and it provides natural opportunities for both movement and stillness.

To begin developing audience skills with your group have half the group perform the poem while the other half watches. Remind the audience that their job is to watch and listen attentively. When the performers are finished, allow the audience to give them positive feedback on their performance. You can encourage this by cueing them with questions such as *"What was you favorite part of the poem? What made that part exciting for you? How did they show us that they were tigers?"* Be sure to reverse roles so that everyone in the class has a turn to be both performer and audience member. (Also see Lesson 11, Commentary, for more about sharing with an audience.)

VARIATIONS:

To encourage composition skills, ask your students to come up with words for other parts of a cinquain. At the kindergarten and first-grade levels, it will work best to do this as a whole class, with you providing guidance and writing words down as children express them verbally.

Use the cinquain form to enhance other areas of your curriculum. It is possible to write a cinquain on almost any topic, from families to outer space. Have the students perform the poems as in the activity above or ask them to create drawings to go with them.

Lesson 13
Reflection and Sharing

Reflection and Sharing: *TV Interview* (15–20 min.)

Reflection and Sharing: *TV Interview*

CONTEXT:
"We're going to be interviewed about our Journey for a TV news show."

SKILLS:
Awareness and expression of inner thoughts, feelings, and values
Public presentation: the outward expression of inner thoughts and feelings

MATERIALS / PREPARATION:
- Before the class arrives, set up the area where individuals will stand to be interviewed, including the following:
  - carpet square, platform, sturdy box, or other way to designate a small "stage" for interviews
  - microphone, either real or pretend (such as a toy or a decorated cardboard tube)
  - instrument for recording the interview: a video camera or a tape recorder or a pen and paper

- (Optional) You can arrange in advance to have another adult — in role as the TV camera crew — videotape the interviews.
- Prepare a list of interview questions based on the kinds of learning you want your class to experience. (For more about asking questions related to teaching goals, see Commentary at the end of this lesson and the section, Asking Questions in Chapter 2.)
- Initially, you will receive a telephone message that will set the stage for this lesson. You have the option of arranging in advance with another adult to call you on your classroom telephone or to send you a telephone message from the office. (You

---

can also choose to simply announce to your class that you have received a telephone message.)

PROCEDURE:

1. You receive a telephone message (the telephone rings or you receive a note from the office). Announce to your class:

"A local television station has called us, (name of your photography company). *They have heard from the Sierra Club about our Journey and want to interview us for TV! They're coming over right now!"*

2. Show students the interview stage and microphone. You or another adult will play the Interviewer. Students will answer questions in their role as professional photographers. Encourage all students to participate, but if some students are reluctant to speak, allow them to simply watch.

   One way to set up the interview is to have students line up at the stage when they want to answer a question. Students will then step up to the stage one at a time to answer questions. An alternative format is to have all students sit in a circle. After each question is asked, pass the microphone around the circle so that everyone gets a turn to answer. Students may say, "Pass" if they don't want to speak.

3. Begin the interview: Ask a question and allow several students to answer before continuing with the next question. This allows students to compare and contrast their answers with the answers of others. (See list of suggested types of questions at the end of this section.)

4. When the interview session is over, place the recorded answers — on video or audio cassette or in writing — in the Time Capsule.

INTERVIEW QUESTIONS:

The following is a suggested list of types of questions appropriate for *TV Interview.* Your own questions may look quite different. The words in **bold italics** are particularly useful phrases for eliciting reflective answers.

To encourage students to interpret their experiences of the Journey and to select significant points:

> *"What was the most important part of your Journey?"*

> *"What would you like to tell your family about your Journey?"*

To encourage students to consider alternatives:

> ***"What do you think might have happened if*** *you had brought the tiger back home with you?"*

> ***"What do you suppose would have happened if*** *the group had become lost?"*

To imply importance of students' actions beyond their immediate personal concerns:

> ***"What do you imagine*** *the children of the future will think when they find your Time Capsule?"*

> ***"Do you think*** *your photographs will help endangered species?"*

To ask for a personal response, regarding either the experience itself or students' relationships to others:

> ***"What were your concerns when*** *you saw that Annie had been hurt by the tiger?"*

> ***"Were you in agreement*** *with the group decision to capture the tiger?"*

> ***"What was on your mind when*** *you first arrived at base camp?"*

> ***"What were you thinking about when*** *you received your award?"*

To encourage students to make value judgments:

"*Do you think it was right to* capture the tiger in the first place?"

"*Was it wise to* leave Annie and Robert alone when the group went to capture the tiger?"

To clarify for the teacher:

"*Do I understand you to mean* that you disagreed with the group's decision to let the tiger go?"

"*Are you saying that* you would capture the tiger differently next time?"

COMMENTARY:

This lesson creates a formal yet nonthreatening way for students to speak their private thoughts, feelings and experiences in public. Public speaking requires clarity of language, good stage presence, and a clear voice that is loud enough to be heard by all. Giving students the option of not speaking creates a safe atmosphere for them to contribute freely, without pressure. By using a structured format — making a single-file line at the interview stage or passing the microphone around the circle, you assure students that all will receive a fair turn.

Carefully prepare your interview questions beforehand. Reread the section on Asking Questions in Chapter 2 and be clear about your educational goals for this lesson as you formulate your list of questions. The TV Interview has been placed at this point in the curriculum to give students the opportunity to interpret and evaluate their Journey drama, and for the teacher to monitor any changes in the students' learning process as a result of the Journey experience.

In order for students to feel they can speak freely, do not evaluate their responses. Take care to not imply value judgments or an expectation of a "right" answer in your role as Interviewer. Be aware of nonverbal signals you may be giving in your body language and vocal intonation. Maintain a safe atmosphere for answering questions by using the bland, subjective, nonemotional wording and vocal intonation of a TV interviewer. Don't rush students to answer questions immediately — give them time to think.

VARIATIONS:

Individual students can take a turn playing the Interviewer. Although their questions may not be as focused as those on your carefully planned list, the experience of asking questions will help them develop communication skills.

Formal interviews can be used to discover what your students know or understand about any topic. For example, after a field trip to see a play, students can be interviewed about what they remember and understand about the play. Or, after a class discussion about classroom rules, students can be interviewed about both the rules and the discussion process.

Public Sharing Event

A. Public Sharing Event   (15–20 min.)
B. Sealing the Time Capsule   (5 min.)

At this point in the drama curriculum your students are ready to show some of their drama activities to others. Plan an event in which your students can share some or all of the drama forms they've created in Part IV with a small group of people, such as another class. This public sharing should be an informal and enjoyable gathering, with the emphasis on creating a positive experience for the participating students (as opposed to a stressful performance).

A. *Public Sharing Event*

CONTEXT:
"Members of the Sierra Club are coming to observe the results of our Journey."

SKILLS:
Public presentation: the outward expression of inner thoughts and feelings

MATERIALS / PREPARATION:
- A ribbon long enough to wrap around the Time Capsule box and tie in a bow, or some other item, such as tape, for sealing the Time Capsule
- See below for each activity

PROCEDURE:
1. Make arrangements for another class to visit your classroom. (See Variations regarding inviting students' parents to your sharing event.)

   Inform the teacher of the visiting class about your Journey experience. The visiting class will be present as members of the Sierra Club who have come to see the results of the Journey experience

---

created by your class' professional photography company. (The visiting students do not need to know more than this, nor are they required to act a role.)

2. Tell your class that members of the Sierra Club are coming to observe your photography company's records of the Journey. Decide with your class which of the following activities they wish to share and make all necessary preparations.

LIVE ACTION:
Title: *Slide Show* (Lesson 11)
MATERIALS / PREPARATION:
- List of slides
- Space arranged for both performers and the audience members
- Rehearsal (if needed)
  (Note: You may want to present the Slide Show twice — each time with half of your class participating, as you rehearsed it in Lesson 11.)

Title: *Animal Cinquain* (Lesson 12)
MATERIALS / PREPARATION:
- Poems, with brief description of movement
- Space arranged for both performers and the audience members
- Rehearsal (if needed)

RECORDING:
Title: *TV Interview* (Lesson 13)
MATERIALS / PREPARATION:
- Video or audio cassette of interviews (or written record)
- VCR and TV monitor or audio cassette player
- Written list of interview questions (optional)

DISPLAY: Placed on tables or tacked on bulletin boards.
  Original letter from the Sierra Club
  Students' passports
  Map of the Journey
  Awards from the Sierra Club
  "Photographs" created in Lesson 10

Time Capsule box
Student drawings of slides
Other artifacts and artwork created by students about the Journey

3. Plan questions and comments for each activity that will direct the attention of the audience to the effectiveness of your students' words and actions (see Commentary, below).

ON THE DAY OF THE PUBLIC SHARING EVENT:

1. When the visiting class arrives, welcome them as members of the Sierra Club and introduce your class as a company of expert photographers. Briefly describe the Journey to observe and photograph animals in the wild and the creation of the Time Capsule.

2. Show any or all of the activities developed in Lessons 11, 12, and 13. During the sharing of these drama forms, direct the attention of your audience with comments and questions (see Commentary, below). This is also an opportunity to instruct about the proper etiquette for being audience members.

3. At the end of your sharing, have your class gather in the performance area and ask the audience for comments and questions. Call on your own students to answer questions from their visitors — they will enjoy being the experts and will have the opportunity to practice public speaking skills.

4. Describe for the visiting class any of the various items you have on display and invite your visitors to walk around your classroom examining the items. Your own students may be available to describe items and answer questions.

B. *Sealing the Time Capsule*

1. After the display items have been freely examined and before your visitors leave, gather everyone together near the display items. Announce that members of the Sierra Club will officially witness the sealing of the Time Capsule. With assistance from members of your class, ceremoniously seal the box. The seal should be tied in a simple bow so that students will be able to untie it later (in Lesson 15).

2. Place the Time Capsule where students can see it for a while before you hide it in preparation for Lesson 14.

COMMENTARY:

Review the Commentary for Lesson 11 in order to prepare yourself for directing the attention of audience members toward certain aspects of your students' presentation. You will want your visitors to observe how effectively your class is communicating their ideas through movement, facial expression, and words. Plan what you will ask the audience to focus on for each activity; for example, *"In the next slide, see if you can tell from the expressions on their faces what the travelers might be thinking."* Or, *"Notice in the next cinquain how the movements match the descriptions of the animals."*

You will also be asking the audience for comments at the end of each activity. Plan to ask questions that will maintain the focus of the audience on the effect of the actions and words of your students, such as: *"Were you able to hear and understand all the words spoken in the interview?"*

VARIATIONS:

You may choose to invite students' parents to your public sharing event. If so, it may be best to plan an evening event, as some students may be disappointed if their parents are not able to come during the work day. Keep the event informal and low-key so that students do not feel under pressure — remember that the purpose of the event is to *inform* parents about your drama curriculum work, not for students to perform for them.

Part VI
NEW PERSPECTIVES

In this section students change their perspective by taking an imaginary trip to the future. Using the drama elements of sound, movement, improvisation, role drama, and story creation students are challenged to think divergently by taking the point of view of people in a future time, looking back to the past (our present time).

In Lesson 14, *Pegasus: Timeship to the Future* students use expressive sound and gesture in response to the story of a ride on a spaceship. When they arrive in "the future," they use their imaginations to improvise a scene, speculating about what the world of the future might be like. In Lesson 15, *Feather, Bone, or Shell,* students again change their perspective by playing the role of people of the future who make up stories about animals of the past. In this role students also search for the Time Capsule and examine its contents.

Lesson 14
Journey to the Future

A. Sound & Movement Story: *Pegasus: Timeship to the Future*
    by Pamela Gerke   (5–8 min.)
B. Imagining: *Future World*   (10–15 min.)

A. Sound & Movement Story:
Pegasus: Timeship to the Future

CONTEXT:
"We will now travel to the future in a special spaceship to see if the children of the future can find our Time Capsule."

SKILLS:
Expressive use of voice (nonverbal)
Expressive use of body

MATERIALS / PREPARATION:
- You will need plenty of space for movement. When the story begins, you and your students will sit together facing each other on the floor in a circle, as if in a circular spaceship. Students will need to be able to see you and to have enough room to make hand and foot gestures while remaining seated.

  When the *Pegasus* takes off after the countdown, you and your students will "fly" through the room and eventually land in an area that will be "the future." You can decide beforehand where the landing area will be or you can simply follow the students' choice of where to land. (There need be no special setup of the room for "the future.")

- Make a sign by taking a piece of cardboard or construction paper and folding it in half so that it stands up by itself. Write on the sign, *"Pegasus:* Timeship to the Future" and include a picture of a flying horse. You can draw the picture or use a magazine picture of a horse onto which you paste a paper cut-out pair of wings. Place the sign in the center of the "spaceship," where you will begin the story.

- Photocopy the "Flight Instructions" (below) for easier handling. Leave the instructions near the sign, where students can find them.
- Place the Time Capsule somewhere where students won't see or find it (in Lesson 15 students will hunt for it while they are "in the future.")

PROCEDURE:

1. When students arrive allow them to discover the Pegasus sign and the Flight Instructions and encourage them to speculate about these items. Explain to students that Pegasus is a special spaceship that travels through time.

2. Invite your class to go on a trip to the future in order to find out if the children of the future have found your Time Capsule. Instruct students to sit in a circle.

3. Tell students that this will be a Sound Story and go over the rules for the sound signals, below.

   Sound Signals:
   - **Make a fist = off**
   - **Open hand, spread fingers = on**
   - **Hand raises up toward ceiling = volume increases**
   - **Hand lowers down toward floor = volume decreases**

   Have students practice following your signals. Demonstrate all the signals while students make these vocal sounds: a running motor, the sound of brakes screeching.

4. Explain to students that in addition to making the sounds, they will also pantomime the actions in this story while remaining seated. Using the sound signals, have students practice doing simple movements while making vocal sounds: pantomime steering

a car steering wheel while making motor sounds; pantomime pressing a foot brake pedal while making the sound of brakes.

5. Read the story, *Pegasus: Timeship to the Future,* using the sound signals as needed. Pause at the end of each of the Flight Instructions while students make the appropriate sounds and gestures. If at any time the making of sounds goes beyond your comfort level or becomes too loud for students to hear the next part of the story, simply use the "off" sound signal: make a fist. Feel free to embellish or change the story as you like. You should not make the sounds yourself, instead allowing students to experiment freely with sounds and gestures.

Pegasus: Timeship to the Future by Pamela Gerke

FLIGHT INSTRUCTIONS:
Welcome aboard *Pegasus!* This ship is named after a flying horse, found in ancient stories called *myths*. To make your trip comfortable and safe, please follow all the instructions carefully. When *Pegasus* takes off you will fly across the room and travel through time to the future. Happy travels!

1. Buckle all seat belts and shoulder harnesses with a sharp "click" sound.

2. Test the alarm system by turning on all the switches:
   a. Siren #1 will sound like a horse neighing.
   b. Siren #2 will sound like a hawk screeching.

3. Turn the big key in front of you. When the engines first fire up, they will sound like a horse who is panting and blowing through its lips.

4. Find the colored buttons marked, "Wing Flaps."
   • Press each one, one at a time. *(Each one will make an electronic sound.)*
   • The wings will now slowly unfold with a soft, hissing sound.

5. While you remain seated on the launch pad, test run the wings of *Pegasus*. They will flap, like the wings of an eagle beating against the wind.

   (Students may flap their wings and create sounds while remaining seated. After ten or more seconds, give the "off" signal.)

6. Prepare for takeoff. When you take off, you will stand up and fly across the room, through time.

   WARNING: When you arrive in the future, **STOP**.
   To avoid jet lag, **SIT DOWN** immediately.

   Countdown: 10–9–8–7–6–5–4–3–2–1–TAKEOFF!!!

   (You and students fly through the room, improvising sounds and movements for 20 seconds or more. Carry the Flight Instructions with you. When you want students to stop, say: "The computer screen says we are now in the future and we must STOP immediately." *)*

   (You and students stop and sit down, as per the above warning. When all students are seated, give the "off" signal.)

7. When you first arrive in the future, the engines will automatically shut off and it will be totally silent.

   (Allow 5 or more seconds of silence.)

8. When the engines have cooled:
   • Press all the colored buttons marked "Wing Flaps," one at a time. *(Each one will make an electronic sound.)*
   • The wings will now slowly fold up, hissing softly.

9. Unbuckle all seat belts and shoulder harnesses with a sharp "click."

10. When you are ready to see the future, exit *Pegasus*.

    (Go immediately to Activity B.)

B. Imagining: *Future World*

CONTEXT:
"We are now many years in the future. What do you see?"

SKILLS:
Use and development of flexible thinking and spontaneity
Understanding and expression of setting (includes time, place, and situation)

PROCEDURE:
1. Together the class pantomimes exiting *Pegasus*. Students can now walk around if they like, while you ask them to imagine the world in the future. Ask questions such as:

   "What does it look like? What sounds do you hear? What kinds of animals do you see? Are there any other life forms here?"

   Encourage students to freely contribute their ideas of an imagined future world. This is more of a talking activity than a movement activity and if students are moving more than you feel comfortable with, you can ask them to sit down while the group imagines the future world. (See Variations, below, to add more movement to this activity.)

2. Tell students that they will now meet people or animals of the future. Choose one or two volunteers to play the roles of the first people or animals that your class meets. Have the volunteers step aside from the group for a moment to think about what they will look and sound like as people or animals of the future. Then have them enter the scene. Allow time for a brief improvisation that need be nothing more than all characters saying "hello" and "good-bye" to each other. Repeat as many times as needed so that all students who desire to have a turn being a person or animal of the future can do so.

3. When you are ready to end the lesson, tell students that in the next lesson (the following day, or whenever you plan for it to happen) they will all be people of the future.

COMMENTARY:
Until this point in the curriculum students have experienced activities from the perspective of people observing animals and of animals being observed by people. In this lesson they take on a new perspective by altering their time frame. This perspective opens up all kinds of creative possibilities for imagining.

Most students will enjoy the opportunity to play with the ideas of spaceships, space, and time travel. Challenge students to avoid stereotyped images from the media, much of which are oriented toward combat and aggression. Encourage students to be thoughtful and creative about imagining people or animals of the future rather than relying on clichés.

Being able to imagine "what could be" is key to developing a sense of hope and to combat despair in the face of what is. Building belief in a positive future is crucial for children today who are growing up in a world threatened by environmental pollution, the extinction of species, a tremendous national debt, and nuclear weapons. Studies show that people who can imagine a hopeful future have a greater success rate for such things as going on to college or surviving cancer and other life-threatening illnesses than people who cannot imagine a positive future.

For more information about legends of *Pegasus,* see Greek Myths: Pegasus, Medusa, Arion-Demeter-Heracles, Perseus, Bellerophon, Zeus and Pegasus, the Pegae (water priestesses of Pirene in Corinth), Aganippe (Demeter as "Night-Mare"), Hippocrene ("horse well" on Mt. Helicon, home of the Muses), and Eos (Aurora).

VARIATIONS:
To invite more creative possibilities for movement and imagination, the flight of *Pegasus* can take place in other locations besides your classroom, such as in different parts of your school building, on the playground, or at the local park. In order to keep the group focused

and cohesive, instruct students to follow you when the timeship takes off. You can preplan the route of *Pegasus* and where you will eventually land, and perhaps have a few surprises prepared for students, such as mobiles of planets and stars hanging from trees or some "futuristic cookies" waiting to be discovered.

Future World is a type of drama activity called, "What If." You can play other "What If" situations with your class by posing a question as a stimulus for discussion, pantomime, or improvised scenes. For example, *"What if our classroom was filled with chocolate pudding? How would we travel across to the other side?"* Or, *"What if you had all the money you wanted. What would you do with it?"*

Lesson 15
Imagining the Future

A. Story Creation: *Feather, Bone, or Shell*   (5–10 min.)
B. Treasure Hunt: *Search for the Time Capsule*   (10–15 min.)
C. Sound and Movement Story: *Pegasus Returns* (5 min.)

A. Story Creation: *Feather, Bone, or Shell*

CONTEXT:
"Today we are people of the future. We have found an object related to an animal of the past and will make up a story about it."

SKILLS:
Collaboration and negotiation with others
Story creation

MATERIALS / PREPARATION:
- You will need one or more objects related to animals, such as a feather, bone, or shell. You may only need to use one object to create a story, but we recommend you have a few more objects on hand in case your class' collective imagination gets stuck or the group wants to make up an additional story.
- If you are planning to immediately follow Activity A with Activity B (*Search for the Time Capsule*) see Materials / Preparation for that activity.
- Begin by having students sit in a circle on the floor, facing each other.

PROCEDURE:
1. From the very beginning of this activity, you and your class will be in role as people of the future. Begin by saying something that will indicate this to students:
   "Welcome to the year 3001 AD. Today we're going to talk about a time of long, long ago: the year _____ (current year)."

2. Tell students that an object from the past has recently been discovered nearby. Place your first object in the center of the circle.

   "Remember that we don't know very much about the past and about the animals that lived at that time. Let's make up a fantastic story about the creature that this object belonged to, way back in _____ (current year)."

3. Guide students in making up a story about an animal of "the past." Students may freely contribute their ideas. The story can be either true-to-life or a fantasy. The following is a suggested procedure for group story creation:

   • Ask questions to begin the story and to stimulate students to imagine details about the animal the object came from, for example:

   "Who knows what kind of creature this feather belonged to?"

   "Does anyone know how this feather ended up here?"

   "What's the first thing that happens in a story about this creature?"

   • As the story develops, continue to ask questions as needed to help motivate and structure the story, for example:

   "I wonder what this creature looked like...what color it was...how big it was?"

   "Describe the kind of place it lived."

   "What do you suppose the creature did first in our story?"

   "What happened next?"

   "What was it thinking...what did it say....where did it go?"

• Students may spontaneously say their ideas out loud. Meanwhile, in a continuing narration, you clarify suggested ideas and incorporate them into the storyline as it develops, recapping events as needed, for example:

"So, the bird was angry and told the people they couldn't have her feather. What did the people say?"

"After that, the people turned into birds and flew away. Where did they go?"

You may have to politely discard any suggested ideas that contradict other ideas that have already been incorporated into the story. You will have to use your best judgment to choose which ideas to include and which to discard without making any students feel slighted.

The story need not be long, have a well-developed plot, or be factually accurate. This is an activity in imagination and collaboration, and you can allow ideas to flow. At the same time, be aware of creating a beginning, middle, and end of your story.

4. Repeat with another object, if desired.

5. Go immediately to Activity B.

COMMENTARY:
There is great value for all artists in what writers call "fluency" or "being capable of flowing." In this lesson it is the imagination that can flow unfettered, much as it does in brainstorming. That's why we suggest that you allow students to spontaneously speak their ideas out loud, rather than having them raise their hands or take turns around the circle — creativity is not always orderly and ideas don't appear only when a child is called upon. If you can allow for a little bit of excited energy, your class will be able to experience fluency in story creating.

The danger, of course, is that the most outspoken, aggressive students will dominate the story creation. Encourage all students to contribute and make sure you are incorporating everyone's ideas. If you choose to have students take turns around the circle, you can allow students to say, "Pass."

VARIATIONS:

You can use any kind of object to stimulate an original story with your class, including objects that relate to other subjects your class is studying. For example, if you were preparing for a field trip to your local natural history museum you could use a replica of a dinosaur skull as your story stimulus. Or, if your class was going to meet with a visual art specialist you could stimulate a story with a painting or sculpture.

B. Treasure Hunt: *Search for the Time Capsule*

CONTEXT:
"As children of the future you will now search for the Time Capsule from the past."

SKILLS:
Ability to focus attention
Use and development of powers of observation

MATERIALS / PREPARATION:
Hide the Time Capsule before students arrive. Place the box in a place where you think students will be able to find it after spending 5-10 minutes searching for it. You may want to hide it in a place other than your classroom, such as in another part of the building or on the playground. You can also create a trail of clues to lead students to the Time Capsule (see Variations, below).

PROCEDURE:
1. Tell students that long ago, back in _____ (the current year), a Time Capsule was placed somewhere nearby by children of the past. Today, your group will search for the Time Capsule box.

2. Establish with students any rules you've decided upon for the Hunt, such as having students hunt in pairs or small groups, or giving them a time limit. Tell students that when the Time Capsule is found, it must not be opened until the entire class has gathered around it, so that everyone can open the box and examine its contents together. Also explain the boundaries of the area where the Time Capsule is supposed to be.

3. Students search for the Time Capsule.

4. When the Time Capsule has been found, remind students that they are children of the future by saying something from the perspective of a citizen of a future time, such as:

"This Time Capsule was created for us many, many years ago. I wonder what it can teach us about the past?"

Allow students to open the Time Capsule and examine its contents, speculating about the various items. Ask questions to prompt students to imagine the point of view of a person of the future who is ignorant about the contents of the Time Capsule. Encourage students to think creatively and from another perspective, using questions and statements such as:

"I wonder what this map is for..."

"Why do you suppose the people of the past wanted us to find this box?"

"Notice these old-fashioned slides and photographs. Nowadays, how do we take pictures?"

"I see slides of animals in here. Which of these animals are now extinct?"

"Look at what funny clothes these people wore!"

5. When you feel your class has explored the Time Capsule enough for the day, place it somewhere in your classroom where interested students can examine it further.

COMMENTARY:

This activity offers students another opportunity to use their imaginations from the perspective of the future, thus encouraging them to think divergently. By examining their own creation — the Time Capsule — from this point of view, students can examine how they have communicated their ideas and experiences through language and pictures.

VARIATIONS:

If you or a parent volunteer are really adventurous, you can set up a whole series of clues to lead students on a hunt for the Time Capsule. One way to accomplish this is to draw pictures or write words on pieces of colored paper, each clue designating the area where students are to search and eventually find the next clue, ultimately leading to the Time Capsule box. With a trail of clues, you can lead your students' search out of your classroom and around your school building or playground, and perhaps to a nearby park.

Another option is to have the students themselves predetermine details of a drama about finding the Time Capsule, including where it will be hidden. This option will actually not diminish the excitement and anticipation of the hunt — it just changes the activity from a pleasurable mystery to a dramatic scene. Have your students discuss and decide — out of role — *where* the Time Capsule will be hidden and *how* they will discover it, including the kind of clues will they have. You can create anticipation if students do not know *when* their clues will appear.

C. Sound and Movement Story: *Pegasus Returns*

Before continuing on to the next lesson of the Drama Curriculum, bring your students back to the present time in the timeship, *Pegasus*. You can do this on the same day you complete Lesson 15 or on another day. You will need the "Flight Instructions" from Lesson 14.

PROCEDURE:
1. Tell students that they are now themselves again — photographers who have traveled to the future and who must now return to the present time. To do this, you will travel in the timeship, *Pegasus*.

2. Have students sit in a circle with you, as they did when they first entered the timeship for Lesson 14. If needed, review the Sound Signals.

3. Repeat the Sound and Movement story of *Pegasus*. When you get to the last instruction, say: "When you are ready to see the present, exit *Pegasus*."

Part VII
DRAMA AND LITERATURE

Drama and literature share the common goal of communication. Literature is dramatic action captured in the printed word, drama is literature come to life. By exploring literature selections through drama, students gain a first-hand experience of the power and purpose of the written word.

By bringing stories and poetry into action, young students begin to understand that words are symbols that hold the key to a world of ideas, events, and feelings. According to Betty Jane Wagner in *Dorothy Heathcote / Drama as a Learning Medium*, "A reader who has discovered what words on a page actually are — distilled human experience — has cracked the code forever. Such a person can translate any text into meaning by bringing to it the understanding, first, that it is indeed a code to be cracked, a script to be interpreted, not for an audience, but for one's own illumination; and, second, that to make sense of it requires the application of one's own experience."

Through drama students are exposed to and come to appreciate literature of many kinds, including poetry and rhyme, folktales and fairy tales, fables and myths, and contemporary children's books, as well as literature written specifically for the theater. Some nonfiction materials, including biographies, also hold rich possibilities for dramatic experience. In becoming personally involved in each selection students internalize its structure, enriching their skills as future composers of language as well as interpreters of it.

As students have moved through *Hooves and Horns, Fins and Feathers,* they have been moving from drama generated by and for themselves toward drama that interprets the words of others. The focus of the lessons in the following section, however, is still on the

169

student's own experience rather than on creating an experience for an outside audience. Although dramatizations of many of the stories and poems may certainly be shared with others, the primary goal is still to encourage students to feel and express belief in an imaginary situation — here, the events in a piece of literature.

In this section of the curriculum, children will be guided to respond to written selections in several ways, including through movement and pantomime, choral speaking of the words, and dramatizing a story with improvised action and dialogue. Each lesson will model one type of response using a specific literature selection, the text of which is included in the lesson. The literature selections we have chosen relate to the theme of animals. Other selections relating to this theme that can be explored using the same procedure are suggested at the end of each lesson. You are, of course, also welcome to use favorite selections of your own.

Exploring literature through drama provides students with opportunities to express and create, to collaborate with others, and to gain a lifelong appreciation for the world of language.

Lesson 16
Literature and Movement

Movement Story: *Life in the Bass Lane* by Pamela Gerke
(15–20 min.)

LITERATURE AND MOVEMENT:
Life in the Bass Lane by Pamela Gerke is an example of a Movement Story — a story that is narrated by the teacher as the students move spontaneously. In a Movement Story, all the children play each of the characters, switching from one character to another as the narration dictates. The purpose of a Movement Story is to encourage full-body expressiveness through pantomime and dance. Movement Stories represent the combining of creative dance and drama.

Movement Story: *Life in the Bass Lane*

CONTEXT:
"Today we're going to move to a poem about wild creatures who live in an ocean environment."

SKILLS:
Use of the whole body in movement
Expressive use of body and movement

MATERIALS / PREPARATION:
- Ideally, when you tell this story to your class you should be able to do the movements along with your students (we encourage teachers to always participate in movement activities). We recommend that you do one of the following:
    - Memorize the story.
    - Photocopy the text (so that it can be easily held in one hand).
    - Write the story in large letters on a big piece of paper that you tape to the wall. This will also allow students to see the correspondence between the written and spoken words.
- CD player or tape deck (music is optional, but highly recommended)

MUSICAL SUGGESTIONS:

A light, carefree selection such as:

John, Esther "Little Dove," "Ocean Bossa," *The Elements, Volume II*

Chappelle, Eric, "Dancing Digits," *Music for Creative Dance: Contrast and Continuum: Volume III*

PROCEDURE:

1. Tell children that they will be going on an undersea adventure, and that some of the story will take place in Self Space, meaning that they will stay in one spot. Have the students explore their Self Space by stretching, swinging, and twisting their bodies while staying in one place. Tell students that other parts of the story will ask them to move around the room that is called moving in General Space. Ask students to travel briefly through General Space by walking, galloping, floating, and turning, then say "Freeze" when you want them to stop their movement.

2. Ask the students to find an empty spot to stand where they can stretch their arms without touching another person. Read the following poem as the children do the described movements. It is highly recommended that you move along with them as much as possible in order to provide a model for the movements.

Life in the Bass Lane: An Undersea Adventure by Pamela Gerke

Walk around the room...then stop!
In your own, special place
Where you can stretch
Without touching anyone:
Your own Self Space.
Feel all around you
An invisible bubble.
  (Use hands to "feel" the space all around you.)

While inside it you can move,
Protected from all trouble.

Now, in your bubble, come with me
And we'll explore the mystery
Of the big, deep, blue sea...

We sink into the water,
  (Slowly sink to the floor.)
Going down, down, down,
To the bottom of the ocean
Where there's hardly any sound.
  (Sit or lie down.)

(Whisper:) Listen to the silence of the ocean...
  (Pause for a few moments of silence.)

In this watery world
We can be
All the living creatures
That we see:

We can be an octopus
  (Begin to move as octopus, waving arms and legs.)
Sitting in Self Space,
Counting all its arms
From number one to number eight:
  (Move arms and legs while counting.)
1, 2, 3, 4, 5, 6, 7, 8.

And there, sitting by itself too,
Is a sea anenome that's purple and blue.
  (Curl up limbs toward the center of your body.)
When it's curled up in a little ball
The anenome is very small.
But when it's hungry it begins to grow

And opens up — slow, slow...
  (Slowly extend arms and legs outward.)
And as it gets bigger in size
It starts to rise and rise...
  (Slowly stand up.)

...Until it sees something to eat,
And goes, "CHOMP!"
  (Pantomime taking a huge bite, grabbing something with your arms.)
Then quickly closes up again,
Small and neat.
  (Resume small, curled-up shape on the floor.)

There's a little, baby sea bass
  (Stand and crouch to make a small shape.)
With a little, fishy face,
  (Make a "fish face.")
Swimming 'round a little rock,
In its own, little place.
  (Crouching in a small shape, "swim" on two feet in a small circle.)

It swims all by itself,
Until it learns the rule:
All little fishies must go to school!

Now we swim in open space
All across the sea.
We each leave our own Self Space
To swim far and free.
  ("Swim" all around in General Space. Encourage children to "swim" on two feet, as well as on their bellies.)

Now a sea bass is very small
Compared to the largest sea creature of all.
Who is the largest?
  (Children say what they think.)

Yes, whales are the biggest creatures in the mighty big sea.
Can you show me how very large
A whale can be?
  (Make a big shape.)

Whales are very sociable
And don't live all alone.
They live in groups called "pods"
In their lovely ocean home.

Can you swim in a big shape
With other big whales,
Without bumping into anyone
With your fins or your tail?
  ("Swim" in general space, keeping big shape.)
  (Music begins.)

Whales called "orcas"
Have a very special flair
For these black-and-white mammals
Like to leap in the air!

Big, giant leaps!
Leaps that are small!
Medium-sized leaps!
And the biggest leaps of all!
Heaps and heaps of leaps!

Orca whales have lots of fun
When they leap and dance
In the air and the sun!
  (Allow for a free dance period of 30 seconds to one minute. Music ends.)

Now dive to the floor
Of this watery place

And find some slippery eels
Slithering silently in Self Space…
   (Sink to the floor and slither on your stomach, silently.)

There're some cranky crabs here,
Scuttling sideways with a sigh.
   ("Crab walk" on hands and feet, sideways.)
They gently bump each other —
"Excuse you!" the cranky crabs cry!

Now is the time:
To the ocean's surface we must climb.
We slowly rise to the top of the sea,
   (Stand up.)
And sway gently in the water's motion,
   (Sway in place.)
We remember all we've seen and we say:
Thank you, wonderful ocean!
We'll come again another day!

COMMENTARY:
It will be helpful to practice the poem before presenting it so that you can speak each verse with a steady meter, which will help the children feel and respond to its rhythm. Feel free to stop between each verse and allow time for the children to move. At these times you can make observations about the children's movements, such as, "*I notice Sarah making a very small anenome shape.*" Or, "*I see Jessie doing huge leaps at a high level.*"

There are two places in the story for silence: when you first go to the bottom of the ocean and near the end when you become eels. Don't cut the silences short — teachers often feel obliged to keep up a steady stream of talk and activity, but they should instead allow time for children to listen in silence.

This story asks students to imagine a bubble around themselves in order to visualize the space that their own body takes up. This space is also called the kinesphere. It's important for young children to develop a sense of their kinesphere in order to maintain control over their bodies as they move in space. Having control over one's own body and movement gives children a sense of both safety and excitement. They can do so many exciting movements with their own body! Anne Green Gilbert, author of *Creative Dance for All Ages*, recommends that when two children bump into each other, both freeze for five counts. During the five counts they can be looking for an empty space in the room to move to.

VARIATIONS:
If you feel that the poem is too long for your class to do in one session, try doing a small section of the poem each day. After each section of the poem has been experienced separately, you can put them all together and repeat the poem on subsequent days as your class desires.

For each of the different sea creatures portrayed here, you can allow time for free dance. Select different music for each sea creature and pause between each section of the poem to play music for free dance. Perhaps you'll use slow, dreamy music for an octopus dance and lively, silly music for a crab dance.

You may further explore poetry and rhyme by asking students to think of rhyming words. For example: You say a simple word, such as "shark," and the children try to rhyme it with words like, "dark" and "bark." When you have a string of rhyming words, the class can make up a poem, such as: "The shark / swam in the dark / and heard the seals bark." You can then ask the students to put their own poem to movement.

Integrate the visual arts by having the students create a mural of undersea life to use as a backdrop for the activity.

Lesson 17
Literature and Choral Speaking

A. "Two Little Blackbirds" by Mother Goose   (10 min.)
B. "The Little Red Hen," Traditional English Tale, retold
  by Helen Landalf   (15–20 min.)

LITERATURE AND CHORAL SPEAKING:

In choral speaking the students chant words or phrases from a poem or story, often in unison. Choral speaking provides an excellent introduction to dialogue because speaking in a group reduces self-consciousness. The simplicity of the chanted phrases in this lesson does away with the need for memorization, which can be a major source of anxiety for students in the realm of public speaking. Louise Thistle, author of *Dramatizing Mother Goose*, says that "Chanting comes from the word enchant. The magical repetition of half singing and half speaking implants the language in the psyche. Children chant when learning new words."

A. Two Little Blackbirds

CONTEXT:
"Today we will use our voices to recite a poem about two black-birds."

SKILLS:
Expressive use of voice and language
Communication (both listening and speaking)

MATERIALS / PREPARATION:
Familiarize yourself with the nursery rhyme "Two Little Blackbirds" by Mother Goose, included in this lesson. The lesson will be most successful if you are able to recite the poem from memory so that you can maintain eye contact with your students throughout the lesson.

PROCEDURE:

1. Recite the poem "Two Little Blackbirds" aloud, modeling the corresponding hand movements.

2. Ask students to recite the poem with you, imitating your hand movements. Repeat this several times, until the students seem familiar with both the words and movements.

3. Have the students repeat the poem several more times, this time with the following vocal variations:

   Whisper, or speak very softly.

   Use a loud voice (but not a shouting voice).

   Speak in a high-pitched voice, like an elf or a mouse.

   Speak in a low-pitched voice, like a giant.

   Recite the poem as quickly as you can.

   Recite the poem very slowly.

Two Little Blackbirds by Mother Goose

Two little blackbirds
Sitting on a hill
   (Hold both fists in front of you at chest level. The back of the hand should be facing outward and fists should be close together.)
One named Jack
And the other named Jill.
Fly away Jack.
   (Mime one hand "flying away," then hide that hand behind your back.)
Fly away Jill.
   (Remaining hand "flies" away, then hides.)
Come back Jack.
   (First hand "flies" back, makes a fist.)
Come back Jill.
   (Second hand "flies" back, makes a fist next to the first hand.)

COMMENTARY:

Doing the hand movements as they recite "Two Little Blackbirds" will help children remember the words of the poem, because their brains will link the words with their corresponding movements. This is why actors often learn their blocking, or stage movements, as they memorize their lines. You can use the principle of linking language and movement whenever you ask your students to memorize something. For example, you might have children make shapes with their bodies while saying each letter of the alphabet, such as making their bodies into the shape of a B when they say the letter B.

Chanting in unison helps students develop a feeling of group unity. Encourage them to listen to the sound of the whole group as they are speaking rather than focusing on their own individual voices. Challenge them to begin and end each word at the same time as everyone else. A tape recording of their voices chanting in unison will be highly motivating, as well as lots of fun for them to listen to.

VARIATIONS:

After the children have recited "Two Little Blackbirds" using hand movements, you can dramatize it further by having two children play the parts of Jack and Jill. Begin the poem with Jack and Jill seated in two chairs at the front of the room. As the rest of the class recites the poem, the two performers can mime the actions of flying away from each other and returning. Be sure to repeat this many times to that everyone can have a chance to play one of the blackbirds.

B. The Little Red Hen

CONTEXT:
"Now you'll use your voices to help me tell a story about a hen, a duck, a mouse, and a pig."

SKILLS:
Understanding and expression of character
Communication (both listening and speaking)

MATERIALS / PREPARATION:
Familiarize yourself with the story of "The Little Red Hen," included in this lesson. This activity will be most successful if you are able to tell the story rather than read it. If you do choose to read the story, copy it onto a single sheet of paper for easier handling.

PROCEDURE:
1. Tell or read aloud the story of "The Little Red Hen."

2. Ask students to say the words "Not I," in unison, in a duck's voice. Encourage them to think about whether the duck's voice would be loud or soft, high or low, slow or fast. Ask them to try putting a "quacking" sound into their voice as they say "Not I." Repeat this process with the voices of the mouse and the pig, drawing your student's attention to the possible ways of expressing the differences between the voices of each character.

3. Retell or reread the story with the students chanting "Not I," in the appropriate places, using the animal voices they have practiced. Remind them that when the Little Red Hen asks if they will eat the bread at the end of the story they will say "I will!" instead of "Not I."

The Little Red Hen
Traditional English Tale, retold by Helen Landalf

Once upon a time a Little Red Hen was in the farmyard with her chicks, looking for something to eat, when she came upon a grain of wheat. That gave her an idea.

"Who will help me plant this wheat?" she called.

The Duck quacked, "Not I."

The Mouse squeaked, "Not I."

The Pig grunted, "Not I."

"Then I'll plant it myself," said the Little Red Hen. And she did.

When the grain of wheat was in the ground, the Little Red Hen called, "Who will help me water the wheat?"

The Duck quacked, "Not I."

The Mouse squeaked, "Not I."

The Pig grunted, "Not I."

"Then I'll water it myself," said the Little Red Hen. And she did.

When the wheat had grown tall and golden and ripe she called, "Who will help me harvest the wheat?"

The Duck quacked, "Not I."

The Mouse squeaked, "Not I."

The Pig grunted, "Not I."

"Then I'll harvest it myself," said the Little Red Hen. And she did.

When the wheat was ready to be ground into flour, the Little Red Hen called, "Who will help me take the wheat to the mill?"

The Duck quacked, "Not I."

The Mouse squeaked, "Not I."

The Pig grunted, "Not I."

"Very well, I'll take it myself," said the Little Red Hen. And she did.

When the wheat was ground into flour, the Little Red Hen called, "Who will help me bake the bread?"

The Duck quacked, "Not I."

The Mouse squeaked, "Not I."
The Pig grunted, "Not I."
"Then I'll bake it myself," said the Little Red Hen. And she did.

When the bread was baked, the Little Red Hen called, "Who will help me eat the bread?"
The Duck quacked, "I will!"
The Mouse squeaked, "I will!"
The Pig grunted, "I will!"
"No, you won't!" said the Little Red Hen. "I'll do it myself. I earned this bread, and my chicks and I will eat it up!" And they did.

COMMENTARY:

This lesson gives students an introduction to using variations in vocal quality to express specific characters. The words *quacked, squeaked,* and *grunted* will help children naturally create appropriate voices for each animal. As the students gain further practice in speaking as characters their vocal expression will become increasingly sophisticated and imaginative.

VARIATIONS:

You can experiment with substituting other animals for the Duck, the Mouse, and the Pig in this story. For example, you might change the characters to the Cat, the Dog, and the Snake, or the Bear, the Wolf, and the Eagle, or even the Whale, the Elephant, and the Dinosaur. You may also decide to substitute a different animal for the Little Red Hen, as well as describe a task other than growing and harvesting wheat. As in step #2 of the Procedure, have the students practice saying "Not I" in the voices of any animals you will be using in the story.

Rather than having all the students play each animal, divide your class into three groups, with one group being the Duck, one group being the Mouse, and the remaining group being the Pig. Each group will chant "Not I" only when it is their animal's turn to speak.

Integrate word recognition by creating printed signs, one with the name of each animal in the story. Hold up a sign that says "Duck," for example, when it is the Duck's turn to say "Not I." After several repetitions of the story your students will begin to recognize the signs.

Add vocal variations to any words or phrases you traditionally have the students chant together in your classroom. For example, have them try whispering the alphabet, or saying the days of the week like a duck.

OTHER SELECTIONS FOR LITERATURE
AND CHORAL SPEAKING:

Many Mother Goose rhymes may be spoken chorally. The advantage to using these rhymes is that most children are familiar with them, making memorization unnecessary. *Dramatizing Mother Goose* by Louise Thistle contains the text of many rhymes along with suggestions for accompanying movement.

Brown Bear, Brown Bear, What Do You See? by Bill Martin, Jr. and Eric Carle is a classic children's picture book that is ideal for choral speaking. The children chant a repeated question, such as *"Brown Bear, Brown Bear, What Do You See?"* and the teacher replies: *"I see a red bird looking at me."* In each repetition of the chanted line, children use the name of the animal who replied, in this case: *"Red Bird, Red Bird, What Do You See?"* The same format is used in *Polar Bear, Polar Bear, What Do You Hear?*, also by Martin and Carle, and in the children's book *I Went Walking*, written by Sue Williams and illustrated by Julie Vivas.

Owl Babies, written by Martin Waddell and illustrated by Patrick Benson, is the story of three baby owls whose Owl Mother seems to have disappeared. Sarah and Percy owl speculate on where she might have gone and what she will bring back, but little Bill can only say, "I want my Mommy!" Children will greatly enjoy chanting Bill's plaintive line as you read the story.

Lesson 18
Literature and Improvisation

Story Dramatization: "Deep in the Forest" by Brinton Turkle
(25–30 min.)

LITERATURE AND IMPROVISATION:

Up to this point, the Drama and Literature section of this curriculum has focused on students responding to or recreating the language in a text. In this lesson, students will improvise their own narration and actions based on the events and sequence of a story, in this case the wordless picture book, *Deep in the Forest* by Brinton Turkle. *Deep in the Forest* is a reversal of the story "Goldilocks and the Three Bears," for it shows a little bear coming upon a human habitation in the woods. As there are no words, you will need a copy of the book — readily available in most public libraries — in order to present this lesson.

The book opens with a little bear coming upon a cabin in the woods. He creeps in the door, then walks to the table upon which are three bowls, labeled "Papa," "Mama," and "Baby." He tastes from Papa's bowl, then Mama's bowl, and then Baby's bowl, which he knocks off the table.

Next, the bear tries sitting in Papa's chair, which is hard and uncomfortable. Then he tries Mama's chair, into which he sinks awkwardly. When he tries baby's rocking chair, he breaks it and falls to the ground.

The little bear makes his way into the bedroom, where he bounces on Papa's bed, pulls the feathers from the pillow on Mama's bed, then falls asleep in Baby's bed. When the people of the house come home, they see the bowl on the floor, the broken chair, the feathers, and finally the bear in Baby's bed. They chase the bear from the house. He runs home to his family, where he is comforted by his Mama.

Story Dramatization: *Deep in the Forest*

CONTEXT:
"When we were on our Journey we talked about how an animal might feel to see humans in its home. Today we'll work with a story about how some humans feel to see a bear in their home."

SKILLS:
Expressive use of voice and language
Use and study of dramatic form

MATERIALS / PREPARATION:
A copy of the book *Deep in the Forest* by Brinton Turkle

PROCEDURE:
1. Seat children as you normally would to tell or read them a story. Tell them that the book you will be sharing, called *Deep in the Forest,* has no words. Ask them to notice if their minds say any words as you show them the pictures. Show each picture in sequence, giving enough time for the students to see and comprehend the events in each picture. Both you and your students should remain silent as you share the book.

2. Next, tell the students that they will now help you create words to go with the pictures. Show the first picture in the book and ask *"Who can tell me what is happening in this picture?"* Show the pictures in sequence again, calling on volunteers to describe what is happening in each.

3. Tell children that you will now narrate the story while they act the part of the bear. (Note: If you have a large class, you may choose to have only half of the students act out the part of the bear while the other half watches, then switch roles.) Have all the students go to an open area of the room and pantomime the actions of the bear as you describe the pictures. For example: *"The Baby Bear ate some cereal from the Papa's bowl."* (All

children mime eating out of a bowl.) Do not provide real props such as bowls and chairs; instead, have the students show the objects through pantomime. Continue narrating the story up to the point where the bear crawls into the little bed, just before the humans return.

4. Now, ask a student volunteer to be the narrator. Have the narrator hold the book and describe each picture in sequence from the beginning to the end of the book, as if they were reading the story. Choose three students to play the Papa, Mama and Baby. If you feel that your students may need some extra guidance, you may take the role of Papa or Mama. All other students will play the Baby Bear simultaneously, as before. Allow the volunteer to narrate the story, with the students (and you) pantomiming the actions. The narrator should be the only one who speaks.

5. Repeat the story, as desired, with other students playing the humans and with a new narrator.

COMMENTARY:
The emphasis in this lesson is on the students generating language to describe what they see, not on creating an original story as they did in Lesson 15. It is fine for their language to be very simple, as long as it accurately describes the events shown in the pictures.

Improvising story narration is an excellent prereading activity. Children will enjoy the grown-up activity of "reading" the book page by page, and they will gain an understanding of the sequence of events in a story. Repeat this activity on subsequent days so as many students as wish to will have a chance to be the narrator.

VARIATIONS:
If pantomiming the entire story feels like too large a task for your class, simply do the beginning of the story, before the humans make their entrance. Or, you may decide to do the first section of the story on one day, adding the ending at your next drama session.

After acting out *Deep in the Forest*, your students will enjoy hearing the story of "Goldilocks and the Three Bears." You can discuss what makes the stories similar and what makes them different.

Have the students "narrate" what is happening in other pictures — their own drawings, prints of famous paintings, or photographs from magazines. You can have each student select three magazine photos and put them into a sequence that suggests a story. Then they can tell the story to the class, describing each picture in sequence. It is nice to write the children's words below the pictures as they say them.

If you feel your class is ready, try asking them to improvise dialogue for the story instead of having them simply pantomime the action as you or a child narrates. This may work best after the students are familiar with the story and have pantomimed the actions several times.

OTHER SELECTIONS FOR IMPROVISING
ACTION AND NARRATION:

Good Dog Carl by Alexandra Day is one of several wordless pictures book about a dog named Carl. In *Good Dog Carl*, the dog makes mischief while his mistress is away, but he manages to repair his misdeeds before she returns. In improvising this story have all the students play Carl (the dog), with you or a student playing the mistress. You may narrate the story the first time, then ask for volunteers.

Children can provide narration for any picture book with words in which the illustrations clearly describe the narrative. This improvisation will bring them even closer to the act of actual reading.

Lesson 19
Literature and Dramatization

Story Dramatization: "The Coyote and the Desert Mouse"
by Helen Landalf (30–40 min.)

LITERATURE AND DRAMATIZATION:
Dramatizing a story is one of the most exciting and satisfying ways for children to experience literature. In dramatizing a story, students make it their own by improvising action and dialogue within the structure of the tale. Experiencing a story through drama allows children to emphasize the aspects of a story that they find most compelling. The fact that the actions and dialogue are improvised on the spot rather than preplanned and rehearsed reduces the anxiety that may be present when memorization is required and thus allows students to become more fully involved in the story. Although a story dramatization may be performed for an audience, the emphasis of this activity remains on the experience of the participants.

Story Dramatization: "The Coyote and the Desert Mouse"

CONTEXT:
"Today you will hear the story of two very different animals, and how they became friends. Then you will act out the story."

SKILLS:
Use and study of dramatic form
Understanding and expression of character
Understanding and expression of setting (includes time, place, and situation)

MATERIALS / PREPARATION:
- Familiarize yourself with the text of "The Coyote and the Desert Mouse," included in this lesson. You may either tell the story in your own words — the preferred approach when working with

---

children — or read it aloud. If you choose to read the story, copy it onto a single sheet of paper for easier handling.

- (Optional) You may choose to prepare your students for this story about two desert animals by showing them photographs of desert environments, coyotes, desert mice, scorpions, and cacti.

PROCEDURE:

1. Tell students that they will be hearing a story about two animals that live in the desert — a coyote and a desert mouse. Ask them to listen to find out how the coyote and the mouse become friends.

2. Tell or read aloud "The Coyote and the Desert Mouse," included in this lesson. Be sure to read or tell the story slowly enough to allow for student comprehension.

3. Discuss the story by asking students the following questions:
   a. How did Coyote and Desert Mouse become friends?
   b. How did the story begin? How did it end?
   c. What was the most exciting part of the story for you?

4. Ask all students to stand up and imagine that they are the desert mouse hunting for seeds. Have them pantomime scurrying across the floor of the desert, either on all fours or upright. Repeat this process with the movements of the coyote and the scorpion.

5. Tell students they will now have a chance to act out the story of "The Coyote and the Desert Mouse." As a group, decide where the locations in the story will be in your drama space: Where will Desert Mouse's burrow be? Were will the cactus be?

6. Discuss with students what characters will be included in their dramatization of the story. Choose volunteers to play Coyote, Desert Mouse, the cactus, and the scorpion(s). We suggest that one student play the coyote, one the mouse, one or two students

play the cactus, two or three students play the scorpions, and the remainder of the group play the mouse's family. You may play one of the mice in order to guide the dramatization from within. Note that the gender of any of the animals in the story can be changed.

7. Guide students in acting out the story. Do this by providing a brief narration of the important events, i.e., *"Desert Mouse woke up and scampered out of its burrow,"* allowing the students to pantomime the actions of the story. Allow students to create their own dialogue as much as possible, encouraging them as needed by asking questions such as *"What did the Mouse say to the Coyote?"* It is fine, at this stage, for the dialogue to be minimal. Use the text of the story to guide your students in creating their dramatization. There is no need to read the story as a narrative script — paraphrasing it in your own words is fine.

8. Replay the story as often as desired, with different students playing the various roles. Each time they play it students will become more familiar with the story, and more able to recreate it fully without your guidance. Once students are comfortable with dramatizing the story, allow them to improvise the dialogue and action as much as possible without your narration. At some point divide the group in half with half acting out the story and half being the audience.

9. Ask the audience questions that evaluate the expressive qualities of the performers and the audience's experience of the dramatization. For example: *"How did Donna show that she was a coyote? Did Howard's voice help us know that he was a mouse? How did the cactus show us that they were catching the coyote? What was your favorite part of the story?"* Monitor the student's responses to make sure they provide positive feedback for the performers. Focus the evaluation on the presentation of the story rather than on the skills or shortcomings of particular children.

The Coyote and the Desert Mouse
by Helen Landalf
adapted from Aesop's fable "The Lion and the Mouse"

Desert Mouse lived in a burrow in the desert with his family. He would hide in the burrow all the hot day, then scamper out in the cool of the evening to search for seeds to eat. His mother always warned him not to wander too far from the burrow, because there were foxes and coyotes who loved to eat little desert mice.

Nevertheless, one beautiful evening when the sun had set, little Desert Mouse poked his head out of the burrow, then climbed out and began to search for seeds. Farther and farther from the burrow he went, until he saw what he thought was a gray hill, so up he scampered.

"Aooooow! Aoooooow!" howled the hill, which turned out to be a coyote. Coyote clapped her paw down over the Desert Mouse. "Aha!" Coyote cried. "I shall eat you for my dinner!"

"No, no, please don't eat me," squeaked Desert Mouse. "Please let me go. Maybe someday I will be able to help you."

Coyote laughed at Desert Mouse. "You — help me?" She howled with laughter to think of such a little mouse helping someone as big as she was. "Aooow!" howled Coyote. "Desert Mouse, I admire your courage. I will let you go, but I don't see how you could ever help me."

"Oh, thank you, thank you!" squeaked Desert Mouse, who scampered away as fast as he could go, to the safety of his burrow.

Coyote stalked on through the desert, howling with laughter whenever she thought of Desert Mouse. She was laughing so hard she wasn't watching where she was going and walked right into a prickly cactus. The prickly cactus hung on tight and wouldn't let

Coyote go. The more Coyote struggled to get free, the more tightly she was gripped by the prickly spines of the cactus.

Suddenly Coyote looked down and saw a poisonous red scorpion scuttling along the desert floor, headed right toward her. "Aooow! Aooow!" howled the Coyote. "Somebody help me!"

Deep in their burrow, the family of desert mice heard the coyote's cries. "We must help her!" squeaked little Desert Mouse. So the mice scurried out of their burrow toward the Coyote. They climbed onto the cactus and began pulling at the spines with their teeth. As they pulled, the scorpion came closer and closer, ready to give Coyote a big sting.

Just as the scorpion reached Coyote, little Desert Mouse freed her from the last spine of the cactus. Coyote sprang at the scorpion, howling fiercely, and it scuttled away.

"Thank you," said Coyote to little Desert Mouse and his family. "You have saved my life. Now I know that no one is ever too small to help another." And Coyote and little Desert Mouse were friends forever.

COMMENTARY:

As this lesson is the group's first experience with improvised dialogue, their language may be minimal and they may tend to speak softly. You can encourage dialogue by providing cues such as "...and then Coyote said..." Be sure to give children time to formulate a response, and accept any dialogue they come up with. If there is no response, try coaching the child by whispering lines. Never step in and say lines for a child.

When performing this story for an audience of classmates, encourage students to "share" their words by speaking loudly enough for the audience to hear. This approach is much more effective than telling students to "project their voices," which merely results in the shouting of lines.

Choosing a cast for the first playing of the story is very important. You need to choose volunteers who will model involvement in their roles and enthusiasm for the story. In subsequent playings of the story it is helpful to pair a shy child with an outgoing child in the key roles of Coyote and Desert Mouse.

VARIATIONS:

If you feel that playing the entire story of "The Coyote and the Desert Mouse" will be too much for your class, have them play just one scene. A good choice for this would be the scene where the Mice free Coyote from the cactus. Another alternative is for you to narrate the entire story while the students pantomime, rather than asking them to improvise dialogue.

If you find that your students are self-conscious about playing individual roles, you may cast small groups of children as coyotes and desert mice who can work together in improvising actions and dialogue.

Have the students create a backdrop for the story by drawing or painting a mural of a desert scene on a large piece of butcher paper or on the blackboard.

OTHER SELECTIONS FOR LITERATURE
AND DRAMATIZATION:

Many other Aesop's fables may be dramatized by children. Some favorites are "The Tortoise and the Hare" and "The Grasshopper and the Ant." These fables can be found in any good anthology of children's literature.

Stories to Dramatize by Winifred Ward contains a wealth of literature for dramatization as well as practical suggestions on guiding children in creative drama.

Geraldine Brain Siks' anthology *Children's Literature for Dramatization* is another rich resource for both stories and poetry to dramatize with children from ages five through twelve.

Lesson 20
Literature and Creative Writing

Alternative Endings and Story Dramatization:
"The Secret Night World of Cats" by Helen Landalf
(30–40 min.)

LITERATURE AND STORYTELLING:
Up to this point in the curriculum students have been engaged in interpreting, through pantomime and improvisational dialogue, selected pieces of literature. In this lesson they will use a written text as a springboard for generating their own story-ending ideas. Creating alternative endings for a story helps students understand the kinds of choices a writer must make. Dramatizing a story they have helped to create is highly satisfying for children because they are acting as both generative and interpretive artists.

Alternative Endings and Story Dramatization

CONTEXT:
"Not all animals are wild — many are pets who live happily in the homes of humans. Today you will hear the story of a girl who loses her pet cat. We'll make up our own endings to the story, then act some of them out."

SKILLS:
Story creation / Playwriting
Use and development of flexible thinking and spontanaeity

MATERIALS / PREPARATION:
- (Optional, but highly recommended) A copy of the picture book *The Secret Night World of Cats* by Helen Landalf available in most bookstores. Though the text of the book is included in this lesson, the beautiful illustrations by Mark Rimland will help stimulate storytelling and improvisation.

- Chalk and chalkboard or butcher paper and marker

PROCEDURE:

1. Read Part 1 of *The Secret Night World of Cats* aloud to your students. If you are reading from the book, read from the beginning to the point where Amanda sees twelve pairs of eyes looking at her. End your reading with the words, "'Who are you?' whispered Amanda. 'Why are you looking at me?'"

2. Ask students questions such as the following to stimulate discussion of possible outcomes for the story:

    Do you think Amanda will get away from the eyes? If so, how might she do it?

    Where might Amanda go next in order to find Tabby?

    Will she find Tabby and if so, where might she find her?

    What might Amanda do if she doesn't find Tabby?

    What are some possible ways that this story could end?

   Allow several students to answer each question, listening respectfully and without judgment to each answer. Write the answers on the blackboard.

3. Use several of the answers on the board to create a possible story outcome for the students to dramatize, letting the class know that they will also have an opportunity to dramatize other ideas, as time permits. Write a brief plot summary of the ending to be dramatized, in list form, on the blackboard. For example:

    Amanda runs away from the eyes.

    She goes to the zoo to look for Tabby.

    She finds Tabby in a cage.

    Amanda gets the key and opens the cage.

    She takes Tabby home.

   Read the summary aloud to the students to solidify the alternative story ending they will be dramatizing.

4. Choose one volunteer to be Amanda and one to be Tabby. The rest of the students will play all the other cats in the story. Read

Part 1 of the story aloud again, allowing students to pantomime the actions. When you reach the end of Part 1, continue to narrate the story according to the plot summary created by the class while students dramatize it, improvising action and dialogue as appropriate.

5. Replay the story as many times as desired, trying out several of the alternative outcomes suggested by the students.

6. Conclude the lesson by reading Part 2 of *The Secret Night World of Cats*. Alternatively, you may read the entire story from beginning to end. Discuss with your class how the author's ending differed from the endings created by the class.

The Secret Night World of Cats by Helen Landalf

PART 1

Tabby was Amanda's best friend. They played together every day, and each night Tabby slept contentedly in her little basket beside Amanda's bed. But one moonlit night Amanda awakened to find Tabby's basket empty! So out the bedroom window she climbed in search of her missing cat.

In the cool evening garden behind her house Amanda saw a white Persian cat batting at a tiny silver fish in the pond...a sleek Siamese cat stalking a jewel-winged butterfly...and two calico cats leaping into the air chasing moonbeams. But Tabby was nowhere to be seen. Anxiously, Amanda ventured deeper into the night world to search for her.

Slipping through the garden gate, Amanda entered a dark alley where three lean, hungry alley cats yowled angrily at her from atop a broken fence. Suddenly they began to fight and hiss over a scrap of old fish beside a garbage can.

"I hope they haven't hurt my Tabby!" Amanda thought fearfully. More worried than ever, she began to run swiftly through the streets of the sleeping city and out into the open fields beyond.

"Here, kitty kitty," she called hopefully.

But in the starlit meadow she caught sight only of a tiny golden kitten sniffing a buttercup...a fluffy orange cat listening to the sad songs of night birds...and two young black-and-white cats tumbling in the silver grass. So she ran on through the fields, over a hill and into the dark forest surrounding the city.

Amanda began to move more cautiously, for she knew that the forest was full of magic. Under every curling fern lay a tiny kitten purring and kneading the spongy green moss. An elegant Abyssinian sat proudly on a rock, surrounded by thousands of flickering fire-flies.

Suddenly, in the thick silence of the night Amanda caught a glimpse of Tabby running by! Following her into a clearing, Amanda came upon a wondrous sight: Hundreds of cats dancing in a circle beneath the moon, swaying and weaving gracefully under the stars. Tabby grabbed Amanda's hand, and she found herself whirling, spinning and cavorting in the midst of the dancers. Amanda danced joy-fully, happy to have found her pet. Then she looked more closely at the cat next to her.

"You aren't my Tabby!" she cried as she pulled away from the strange cat's grasp.

"Oh, do stay," implored the cat in a rich, mewing voice. But Amanda was already gone, desperate to find her lost friend.
Amanda ran breathlessly deeper and deeper into the forest until she reached the silent world where giant jungle cats stalk.
"Perhaps Tabby has gone to visit her relatives," she murmured timidly to herself. In the trees just ahead was a lioness resting her

giant chin on huge paws, watching the moon through half-closed eyes. Nearby, her cubs purred loudly as they lapped from a milky stream. In the shadows a tiger's stripes shivered in the night breeze.

Woosh! Amanda ducked just in time to avoid being hit by a flying cat! Hundreds of them sailed from tree to tree like bats.

Then, without warning, the forest became silent. In the silence Amanda felt twelve pairs of yellow eyes glowing at her from behind a thicket. Closer and closer the eyes came, staring at Amanda without blinking.

"Who are you?" whispered Amanda. "What do you want?"

PART 2

But the eyes just kept staring, coming nearer and nearer. Amanda was so frightened that she didn't know what to do...so she began to sing! She sang loud and strong and true. Her voice echoed across the hush of the jungle. As she sang the eyes grew smaller and smaller, disappearing into the darkness.

Amanda felt a soft furry head rub against her leg. She looked down in joyful disbelief.

"Tabby!" she laughed. "Where in the world have you been?" Tabby just swished her tail as if to say "Follow me."

Amanda followed Tabby to the deepest, thickest part of the jungle. Hidden among the creepers and vines was a dark cave. Amanda followed Tabby inside.

"Mew. Mew. Mew." Inside the cave was a tiny kitten crying in sadness as it searched for its lost mother. Amanda watched as Tabby picked up the kitten by the scruff of the neck. She followed as Tabby carried the kitten through the jungle to a hollow tree stump. Inside the tree stump a mother cat lay sadly, fearing she would never see her kitten again. Tabby gently dropped the kitten into the stump beside its mother.

The mother cat's eyes lighted up with joy. She licked her baby, purring loudly.

"Thank you," she said to Tabby in the secret language of cats. Then the kitten and its mother curled up together and slept.

Amanda proudly scooped Tabby into her arms and carried her gently back into the jungle, through the forest, through the narrow alleys and streets of the sleeping city, into the garden and through the bedroom window. Amanda and Tabby slept in each other's arms till dawn, each dreaming of her own special adventure in the secret night world of cats.

COMMENTARY:

Creating alternative endings to a story helps children recognize that there are many possible outcomes to any situation. Creating an imaginative story ending requires divergent thinking — the ability to think "outside of the box" — and is a beginning activity in creative writing, particularly playwriting.

Students will enjoy doing this activity more than once, creating different possible endings for the story. Once they know how it ends in the book, it will be a challenge for them to continue to use their imaginations without being influenced by the author's choices. You can encourage them to think divergently by suggesting unusual possibilities. What if Amanda searched for Tabby at the bottom of the ocean, or in outer space?

VARIATIONS:
You can vary this lesson by stopping at a different point in the story, such as when Amanda joins the circle of dancing cats.

To do this activity as a language arts lesson without the drama element, simply have the students create alternate endings to the story and omit the subsequent dramatization.

Have students decide individually what they would like the ending of the story to be and draw a picture depicting that ending. Students could then share their pictures and ending ideas with the rest of the class.

OTHER SELECTIONS FOR LITERATURE AND STORYTELLING:
This activity can be done using almost any short children's story. Choose a point in the story from which alternative courses of action could branch and ask students to create an ending.

PART VIII

PLAY PRODUCTION:
HOW THE PEOPLE GOT FIRE
BY L.E. McCULLOUGH

Working with Children in Play Production

Ten years of working with children to produce plays, music, and dance performances has shown us that performing can be an enriching, enjoyable, and worthwhile experience for young people and for the adults who teach them. The keys to working on amateur performances are: the attitude of the director, adequate planning, and sufficient rehearsal time so that the performers are confident.

When directing plays with children, we recommend you maintain a positive and calm attitude. Always be fully respectful and supportive of every one of your cast members. It's understandable if you, as director, become anxious and demanding in rehearsals due to your desire to have the production meet your standards of excellence and because of your sense of responsibility for its outcome. However, it will be a more productive and enjoyable experience for everyone if you refrain from expressing anxiety and irritation to your students. Keep the production in perspective: Remember, it's not Broadway — it's a group of kids doing their best and hopefully having fun in the process (we've encountered very few children who didn't absolutely love being in plays).

At the same time, expect nothing but the best from your actors. Demand that they pay attention, cooperate with others, and put forth their best effort. Maintain a rehearsal atmosphere that is disciplined and focused. Be confident in your role as leader and your cast will sense this and react accordingly, respecting your authority and the limits you set. Likewise, if you are unsure of yourself as director your cast will feel insecure, which will then be reflected in their performance.

One of the most difficult aspects of directing children in plays is that they sometimes have a hard time focusing their attention, especially in the beginning. Their excitement about the play may be expressed in boisterous activity, making direction difficult for the adults in charge. Play production teaches children to focus their attention, to work with others, and to take responsibility for their own behavior. Concentrate on teaching your students these skills and remember that they are in the *process* of learning them. Be assured that as rehearsals progress, students will become more able to see how all the parts fit into the big picture of the play and will become more able to concentrate for longer periods of time.

Casting

The following is a suggested method for casting plays with five- to seven-year-olds. We believe that it's neither appropriate nor necessary to audition students at this age. The method described below accommodates all students' choices as much as possible, and students can see that everyone is treated equally.

1. Read or tell the entire story of the play, using either the script or a picture book of the story. Ask the actors to be thinking about which, if any, characters they would most like to play.

2. Ask the actors to say which roles they most prefer and write their choices on the blackboard where everyone can see them. The actors should name all the roles they are interested in playing, even if others have named the same roles. They can also choose to say if they are willing to play any role, or if they prefer a speaking or nonspeaking role.

3. Review the list together and work to complete the cast list to everyone's satisfaction.

- Whenever more than one actor wants the same role, you can pull names out of a hat to make the decision. Children appreciate the fairness of this method.

- The gender of roles can often be changed to accommodate your cast. Make sure to change all the pronouns in the script as needed. Also tell students that it's in keeping with theater tradition for females to play male roles and for males to play female roles.

- Roles can be changed from singular to plural or from plural to singular to accommodate your cast. For example, the role of Coyote could become a Coyote Family, or the Lizard and his Brother can become just one Lizard who is talking aloud to himself.

Script Preparation

After the cast has been determined, make a photocopy of the script. You can then write in any changes (such as pronoun alterations) on this master copy before making copies for the cast. Each actor need only get a copy of the page(s) in which she or he has speaking lines. With a highlighting pen, mark the actor's lines for each copy and send it home with a note to the child's parents or guardians asking them to help their child memorize her or his lines at home. Students can then keep their script pages at home. Copy the entire script and appendixes as needed for other adults who may be helping with your production.

Blocking

Blocking is the planning of all basic stage placement and movement. It is one of the first things you should do in your rehearsal process. Blocking can be tedious, but it's well worth the patience required. Establishing the placement and movement of actors, sets, and props forms a framework for the play and helps to focus the rehearsals. Pay close attention to all blocking of people, props, and sets, and keep accurate notes in your own copy of the script. Each movement affects other parts of the play — a misplaced prop or costume can cause confusion. All the blocking of actors, sets, and props needs to be rehearsed as thoroughly and often as do the speaking lines, so it's best to get started early.

During the blocking process it's often difficult for children to pay attention and remain quiet, especially when they're not in the scene being worked on. In the beginning, they often can't yet understand the big picture and where their character fits in. Over the course of rehearsals all the pieces will come together and the play will jell for them. Until then, don't expect them to pay complete attention when they're not in a scene, and instead set out a quiet activity for them, such as books or drawing materials.

When blocking, use the standard vocabulary for stage directions shown below. Stage directions are from the perspective of the actors when they're facing the audience, i.e., "right" is the actor's right. "Down" refers to the part of the stage closest to the audience and "up" is the part of the stage farthest from the audience.

AUDIENCE

Down Left	Down Center	Down Right
Left	Center	Right
Up Left	Up Center	Up Right

Use many different levels for your stage, such as tabletops or other platforms — a variety of levels makes the staging interesting. If the audience is sitting on the same level as the stage, stage your action as high up as possible, especially if the blocking calls for the actors to be sitting or lying down, otherwise the audience in the back rows will have a hard time seeing.

When planning blocking, be creative with the furniture available to you. Sturdy tables with folding legs can be used as slides by folding up one side of the legs. Slides make for interesting movement and are, needless to say, very popular with kids. Tables, chairs, and other furniture can inspire interesting blocking, as can doors, closets, windows, and other features of the room you use.

Create adequate backstage areas — with enough room for actors, sets, props, and costumes — in places from which the actors can watch the play. If the actors can't see or hear the play, they will swiftly lose interest and focus. It's also more enjoyable for them to be able to watch the show. Make sure you plan the backstage blocking along with the onstage blocking, so that everyone knows exactly where they're supposed to be at all times. If you're working with a large cast, create several backstage areas with a different area assigned to each small group of characters. This will go a long way in maintaining order and quiet.

Use a lot of exciting action that's fun for the kids to perform, and it will be fun for the audience to watch as well. Let them run, jump, skip, fly! Risk a little noise and chaos so that the actors can experience some really exciting movements. Rehearse particularly fast or chaotic action in slow motion first. Always make sure you give clear rules about how to move in the space, and in relation to others, so that everyone is safe.

Repetition in blocking helps children remember what to do (for example, their character always enters from a certain place and exits through a set route). One actor can be assigned to lead group movements, making it easier for the others to follow. Sometimes it's useful for the actors to have an assigned order of movement — who goes first, second, third, and so on — to avoid arguments and to help the actors remember what to do.

Theater Space

The following are a few ideas for being creative with performance space:

- Place the audience around three-quarters of the stage, with your fourth portion being used for backdrops, sets, or backstage.

- Create a theater-in-the-round, where the audience sits in a circle around the stage. The feeling of intimacy can be wonderful and it eliminates the need for large sets or backdrops.

- The entire performance space, including the audience area, can be decorated as the setting of the play, so that the audience is made to feel they are "in" the performance.

- The performance can take place in various locations that the audience must travel to throughout the course of the play, such as the hallway, other rooms, or outside.

Rehearsals

Rehearsals with kindergartners and first graders should generally last between 20–45 minutes, or even up to an hour. Rehearsals can be alternated with production workshops (making the sets, props, or costumes), or with music rehearsals. Always maintain a rehearsal atmosphere that is positive and fun while being focused and under control.

Be open to new ideas generated by students during the first stages of rehearsals. They will most likely come up with great ideas you never thought of, and the actors will feel personally invested in the production if their ideas are heard and, when possible, used. At a certain point, however, you need to establish the artistic decisions so that the play can be rehearsed with consistency and so that everyone can feel secure about what will take place.

After casting and blocking, rehearse individual scenes while creating the production elements (sets, props, and costumes) that are added to rehearsals as they become available. If you don't have all the props available initially, use substitutes so that the actors can get used to them and where they belong. During this time the actors should be memorizing their lines, preferably at home. If they can't remember their lines, encourage the actors to say them in their own words. It's more important that the actors understand what is happening in the story and what their character is intending when they speak than it is for them to say the lines exactly as they are written.

The last few rehearsals should be run-throughs of the entire play. As you get close to the performance day, do a few run-throughs without interruption. Take notes during the run-throughs and go over them with the cast right before the next rehearsal. In addition to your notes, solicit the cast's comments about the run-through and suggestions for future improvements.

For one of your last, dress rehearsals, invite a preview audience. This will go a long way towards helping your actors focus their attention and get past some of their initial nervousness, as well as jelling the play production and working out any problems. At the end of this preview performance, ask the cast to sit on the stage while you solicit the audience's questions and comments. You will be amazed at how much a preview performance will improve your production.

Rehearsal Alternatives

The following are some ideas for fun, alternative rehearsals when you want to make a refreshing change:

- Rehearse the play in fast-forward. Not only is it extremely silly, it's a good way to drill the lines and blocking.

- Run the lines only, while everyone sits or lies down. This is a useful drill and good for when everyone has low energy.

- Do the play in gibberish, so that the actors must express their intent through tone of voice, facial expressions, and gestures. Don't do this if you object to giggling and merriment in your class.

- Switch roles. Seeing what other actors do with their roles can give actors new ideas. It's fine if they substitute their own words for the actual lines.

Basic Acting Skills

At the kindergarten and first-grade level, children should not be expected to be highly skilled actors; however, they are capable of understanding some basic acting skills, including vocal projection and characterization (see suggestions, following). Movement, another basic acting skill, is included in many of the lessons of this curriculum. You can adapt some of these lessons to augment your play rehearsal process. For example, Lessons 1, 2, and 11 have Move and Freeze activities. Here's one way to adapt those lessons to *How the People Got Fire* characters:

1. Call out the name of a character in the play.

2. Give the "move" signal (such as turning on music or playing a drum beat) and ask students to move around the room as that character would move. You can call out suggestions or questions as they move to encourage them to explore their options. For example: *"Lightning makes sharp, jagged movements"* or, *"How does Coyote move when she's about to play a trick on someone?"*

3. At the "freeze" signal (such as stopping the music or drum) students freeze in a statue of that character. Pause for a few seconds, perhaps making observations about what you see.

4. Call out the name of another character and repeat the process.

Other lessons useful for adapting to rehearsals for *How the People Got Fire* include Lesson 3, *Body Part Dance* and *Sculptor and Clay* and Lesson 12, *Animal Cinquain*.

One of the biggest pitfalls of children's play productions is that the actors mumble their lines so that the audience can't hear and understand them. Work with your actors to speak loudly, slowly, and clearly. Help them understand that speaking in a normal, conversational voice will not be effective on the stage. In addition to doing exercises for breathing, diction, and vocal projection, establish your actors' *intention* that the entire audience hear and understand the play. Intention is everything! For example, if you were to see that someone across the street was about to be hit by a car, your intention for them to hear your warning would be very strong and you would automatically have tremendous vocal projection when you said, "Look out!"

Another problem with child actors is that they often merely recite their lines without connecting with the character they are playing. Throughout the rehearsal process, ask your actors about the thoughts, feelings, and intentions of their characters. You can also set up some improvisations of encounters between various characters in the play as well as other scenes that aren't in the script. For example (using characters from *How the People Got Fire*): "*One day, Toyeskom was out flying around and she met Woswosim.*" Or, "*After Skunk sent Thunder and Lightning up to the sky, one day they sneaked back down to earth where the People were having a picnic.*"

Curtain Call and Post-Play Discussion

After the performance, each actor should be able to take a bow by themselves, perhaps with their name and character announced, to receive their well-deserved applause. Any non-acting stage crew members can also be acknowledged, and in the end, the entire cast and crew can take a bow together. Rehearse the bows and maintain onstage quiet and dignity throughout the curtain call, so that each person gets full attention for their bow.

After the curtain call, the cast can sit on the stage for a post-play discussion with the audience. The director solicits questions and comments from the audience and facilitates the actors' answers. Children love showing off their expertise at this time, and both the curtain call and the post-play discussion build self-esteem.

It's nice to end a performance with a reception, or cast party, with snacks and beverages, when the audience and cast can intermingle. You did it!

Production

The following are some general guidelines for creating all the production elements for a play:

- Be creative with your resources — you don't have to spend a lot of money on materials. Paper, cardboard, markers, duct tape, and large fabric pieces can take care of most of your needs.

- Use the production tasks as activities in creating thinking. While giving the actors practical advice on how to make props or sets, allow them to figure things out and come up with their own ideas for construction and design.

- Prepare each task to be as self-directed as possible. If you thoroughly prepare the materials, the actors can work independently. This will free you from the stress of trying to help several groups make things at the same time, or allow you to rehearse with one group while another group constructs sets or props.

- The directions for making sets, props, costumes, sound, and music listed in the appendixes for this script are only suggestions — feel free to use other ideas for creating your own, unique production.

- Sets should be simple and light enough for the children to move by themselves. Large cardboard appliance boxes can be cut to make light, free-standing walls that are good for backdrops. You can tape butcher paper over the wall that students can then paint or color with markers.

- Establish these rules about props with your actors: 1) Props are not toys and should not be played with. 2) Props should only be handled by the actor who uses them and never touched or moved by anyone else. 3) Actors (not the director) should place their own props. Always rehearse with props or prop substitutes.

- A props table can be set up backstage, so that props are not accidentally stepped on or lost.

- Costumes need not be ornate, store-bought, or made by parents. It's possible to simply allow each student to select a colored chiffon scarf or other piece of plain, light fabric. Students can then choose how to wear their scarves as costumes, such as: loosely tied around the neck as a cape, tied around the waist as a belt or skirt, or tied around their forehead as a headband.

- Makeup can be fun but should be optional, for not all children want to wear it and some may be allergic to it. Eye shadow, eyebrow pencil, blusher, and lipstick are easy to obtain and help to emphasize the actors' features. Look for face paints at sale prices right after Halloween.

- Enlist the aid of volunteers to help with your production needs. Many adults enjoy getting involved in play productions, and you will find a wealth of talent and resources among your students' parents. Collaborate with the music and dance/movement specialists at your school to create your show.

Understanding the Dramatic Art: The Meaning Frame and the Expressive Frame

(Thanks to Norah Morgan and Juliana Saxton, *Teaching Drama*)

For the classroom teacher to be an effective drama instructor, it is useful to understand some of the basic forms of the art of drama and theater. Drama can be seen as operating in two frames: the *meaning frame* — the inner understanding, oriented toward the participant — and the *expressive frame* — the outer manifestation, oriented toward the audience. In our first chapter, "Why Drama in the Classroom?" we described the spectrum of drama activities for the classroom, from creative dramatics to theater. Creative dramatics, or process-oriented activities with improvised dialogue and action (including role drama) is primarily concerned with the meaning frame. Theater involves the use of elements and techniques for the purpose of communicating to an audience and can be seen as being primarily concerned with the expressive frame. Play production for public performance is an example of the expressive frame.

Morgan and Saxton have this to say about the relationship between creative dramatics and theater: "Drama and theatre are not mutually exclusive. If drama is about meaning, it is the art form of theatre which encompasses and contains that meaning. If theatre is about expression, then it is the dramatic exploration of the meaning which fuels that expression."

The Elements of Theater

The elements described below are typically associated with theater craft, and a general knowledge of these basic elements is pertinent to a classroom play production. In addition, an understanding of these elements can be applied to other classroom drama activities as well, including creative dramatics, role drama, and story dramatizations. Classroom teachers can make full use of these elements to spark interest, to maintain concentration and motivation, and to crystallize the shared experience of the drama activity. The essential elements of theater craft are: *focus, tension* or *conflict, contrast,* and *symbol.*

In theater, one must **focus** on the big picture — the overall theme or meaning of the play or other work — as well as focus on the parts that make up the whole: the scenes and other details and how they contribute to an understanding of overall theme. Teachers must also focus on both the educational objectives for each lesson and the dramatic focus of the lesson that will further the realization of those objectives. For example, a lesson that has an educational focus of developing awareness and control of body parts may have a dramatic focus of creating a "museum" of statues of animals (see Lesson 3, Activity C, *Replica Museum*).

Tension, also referred to as *conflict,* is the excitement generated in a drama activity or a play that stimulates interest and motivates participants (or, in a play, the characters) to proceed with the unfolding of events. In classroom drama activities, tension is created by challenges, limits on time or space, fear of the unknown, and other factors. Teachers can inject tension into a drama activity by introducing some type of constraint: "We must escape before the guards wake up!" or challenge: "No one has ever returned from that planet — are you still willing to go?" In a play, the conflict is the problem around which the plot revolves (see The Traditional Stages of Play, below) and which creates the tension at the core of the story.

Interest in drama can also be stimulated by using *contrast.* These are the elements that create interest, focus, or tension by virtue of contrast. The contrast of light and darkness can be employed, obviously, by adjusting the lights and window blinds in the room. Equally effective is requiring students to close their eyes and asking them to imagine darkness in the room and to continue to imagine it even after they open their eyes. The contrast of sound and silence can be created with a sound signal (see Sound Stories in Lessons 6 and 14) or by the teacher in role saying something like, "Quiet! I think I hear the spaceships coming!" Movement and stillness can be evoked by a "freeze and unfreeze" signal (see Move and Freeze activities in Lessons 1, 2, and 11) or by the teacher in role: "If we move even a tiny bit the snakes may attack!" Yet another contrast is called peripeteia — the expected and unexpected. Some examples of this contrast include: a powerful warlord who turns out to be a gentle coward, or finding helium balloons at the bottom of the ocean.

Symbol refers to the act of assigning meaning to something, such as a word, an object, or an image. Symbols can have meaning for the collective experience, such as, "This 'talking stick' represents the right to speak in our community." A symbol can also be endowed with meaning by individuals, for example: a "talking stick" might represent the wisdom of the elders for one person, and for another, it represents the power of voice. Symbolization is central to culture and civilization — all artistic endeavors are acts of symbolization.

The Traditional Stages of a Play

As in literature, the essential elements of a play are: *characters, setting* (location and time period), *plot* ("the story"), and *symbol* (see above). In Western culture, plays have traditionally followed a form of four basic stages: *exposition, rising action, climax* and *resolution*. This is not to say that this is the only acceptable form for plays and other types of literature but rather that it has historically proven to be an effective means of telling stories and engaging interest in them. Teachers should be aware of these stages in planning, executing, and assessing drama activities. These stages apply to the role drama, *The Journey,* as well as to the lessons that are more typically associated with theater craft, such as Parts VII and VIII in this curriculum "Drama and Literature," and "Play Production."

Exposition, also called *introduction,* is the part of a play which introduces the primary characters, the setting and the situation. The exposition establishes the conflict or problem that is central to the plot and that motivates the characters to action. In this book, Chapter 6, "Starting Out: Creating a Context," is akin to the exposition of a play for it introduces the context of this drama curriculum and the role drama, *The Journey.*

Rising action, also known as *complicating action,* are the actions and events that arise out of the central conflict or problem of the play and that lead to the climax. In this book, the rising action begins with the invitation from the Sierra Club to photograph animals in the wild, and continues through Parts I, II, and III until the conflict (*Danger!*) in *The Journey, Part 2.*

Climax, also called *crisis,* is the high point of a play, where the central conflict or problem of the play reaches its most dramatic and final turning point. In this book, the role drama reaches its climax in *The Journey, Part 2 — Accomplishing the Mission* and *Danger!*

Resolution, also referred to as *conclusion* or *dénouement,* is the final section of a play in which the conflict or problem is resolved. By this time, the primary characters will have learned something as a result of the conflict/resolution of the story and, ideally, the audience will have gained some new understanding as well. In this book, the role drama reaches its conclusion in *The Journey, Part 3 — Awards Ceremony* and *Creating a Time Capsule.*

How the People Got Fire
script by L.E. McCullough,
edited by Pamela Gerke for this edition

How the People Got Fire is based on a tale from the Maidu tribe of Central California. The Maidu flourished in the coastal country and central valleys north of modern-day San Francisco. They resided in houses made of large earth mounds and lived largely from the bounty of the lush land that surrounded them. The central motif of capturing fire from the gods and bringing it to earth in a flute is widespread in many cultures around the world, recalling the ancient Greek myth of Prometheus, who gave fire to the human race in defiance of the chief god, Zeus. Native American tales about the creation of the world typically use animals as protagonists, emphasizing the human race's dependence upon nature for survival and the belief that animals have spirits, as well.

TIME: The dawn of human history
PLACE: The vast North American desert left by melting glaciers
CAST:
> Narrator (one or more people; can be read by an adult)
> People of the Maidu tribe, including Mother and Child
> Toyeskom — a small bird, ally of the People
> Thunder (traditionally male)
> Lightning (traditionally female)
> 3 Daughters of Thunder & Lightning
> Woswosim — a big bird, ally of Thunder & Lightning
> Lizard
> Lizard's Brother (or Sister)
> Coyote
> Chipmunk
> Skunk
> Other Animals, including: Mouse, Frog, Wildcat, Deer, Snake, Dog, and Fox. (More and other Animals are also possible.)

(Note: Most characters can be played as either female or male. Change the pronouns as needed.)

(Setting: The stage is mostly barren. Scattered about are some medium-sized boulders made of styrofoam or cardboard that actors can sit on and lean against. A campfire is in the center, made of stones in a circle and some kindling sticks. LIGHTS UP. Narrator sits on a rock, on one side of stage. He or she looks at the audience.)

NARRATOR: A long time ago, there was no fire in the world.

(PEOPLE enter, cold and shivering, and sit on the ground on one side of the stage where they huddle in a circle. Some of them carry corncobs.)

NARRATOR: The People who lived in the world then had heard of fire, and they wanted it for keeping warm and cooking their food. They had a small bird named Toyeskom, who had a very bright red eye.

(TOYESKOM enters and is greeted enthusiastically by PEOPLE.)

TOYESKOM: I am Toyeskom, my eye is bright and red; with its shiny glare, I help The People to be fed!

(PEOPLE bring the corncobs to Toyeskom and hold them in front of him.)

NARRATOR: When The People wanted their food cooked they had Toyeskom turn his bright red eye toward the food, and he would stare at it for a long time. The stare from his bright red eye would make the food warm and cook it.

(TOYESKOM kneels, cocks his head toward the corncobs, and shakes and bobs his head as if his motions are cooking the food.)

NARRATOR: But it took a really long time.

(A CHILD steps forward and addresses MOTHER.)

CHILD: Mommy, I am sooooo hungry!

MOTHER: Patience, my child. Our meal will be cooked in a few hours.

PEOPLE: *(Chanting.)* We are The People! We must find fire! We are The People! We must find fire! We are The People! We must find fire!

(TOYESKOM finishes cooking and rises and hands corncobs to PEOPLE, who graciously thank him. PEOPLE can now either sit down in a huddled circle on one side of the stage or exit to change costumes in order to play the ANIMALS.)

NARRATOR: In truth, there was fire in the world but only Thunder and Lightning, who were married to each other, had it. And they would let no one else have any.

(THUNDER and LIGHTNING enter the side of the stage opposite the PEOPLE. THUNDER and LIGHTNING dance and twirl to center stage; they drop several fire embers made of painted styrofoam into the center of the campfire and fall back as the fire blazes up — pantomime or use light effects.)

THUNDER: I am Thunder, Lord of the World! When I speak my mind, The People tremble and fear!

LIGHTNING: I am Lightning, Thunder's Elegant Queen! When I dance through the heavens, my feet paint the evening sky!

NARRATOR: Their daughters kept bits of fire in their aprons, so they would always have plenty.

(THREE DAUGHTERS enter; they each pick up an ember from the fire and put it in their aprons, guarding them carefully. THREE DAUGHTERS and THUNDER and LIGHTNING sit by the campfire.)

NARRATOR: And at night, when darkness fell, a huge giant bird — Woswosim — guarded the main fire and made sure no one got near it.

(WOSWOSIM enters, dancing toward campfire. She carries a spear or club with which she slashes the air and fends off imaginary foes. WOSWOSIM stands guard over the campfire as THUNDER, LIGHTNING, AND THREE DAUGHTERS lie down and sleep. LIGHTS OUT. PAUSE, then LIGHTS UP as LIZARD AND LIZARD'S BROTHER enter and lazily lean up against boulders in another area of the stage.)

NARRATOR: One morning Lizard and his brother were sitting on a rock, sunning themselves. Lizard looked west and was amazed at what he saw.

LIZARD: Brother, look over there! *(Points.)*

LIZARD'S BROTHER: I see. . . smoke!

LIZARD: And where there is smoke. . .

LIZARD'S BROTHER: There is fire!

(They hug each other happily and arm-in-arm march toward center; they stop when they see COYOTE, who has entered.)

LIZARD & LIZARD'S BROTHER: Coyote! Guess what we have seen? Fire!

COYOTE: Fire?

LIZARD'S BROTHER: Smoke, actually.

COYOTE: Smoke?

LIZARD: And where there is smoke...

LIZARD'S BROTHER: There is fire!

(LIZARD and his BROTHER jump up and down excitedly, but COYOTE is unimpressed.)

COYOTE: Listen, Coyote is the Trickster around here. Smoke! Fire! I don't believe a word you lizards say!

LIZARD & LIZARD'S BROTHER: *(Pointing.)* Look!

(COYOTE turns, sees smoke, and is startled.)

COYOTE: It is smoke! And it is coming from the land where Thunder and Lightning live. Quick, lizards, we must call the other animals at once! We must get fire to The People.

LIZARD & LIZARD'S BROTHER: Calling all animals! Calling all animals!

NARRATOR: And in a while, all the animals of the World came: Frog... Fox...Snake...Wildcat...Mouse...Deer...Dog...Chipmunk... Skunk.

(MUSIC: Animals Entrance. FROG, FOX, SNAKE, WILDCAT, MOUSE, DEER, DOG, CHIPMUNK, and SKUNK enter one by one as their names are called, dancing and miming their animal's movements and moving to their places on the stage. They can either stand in a predetermined scattered formation around the stage or form a circle. When all have entered, all can

dance/move together in place or together, moving around in a circle. MUSIC ENDS.)

COYOTE: Animals of the World, we have seen smoke!

LIZARD: And where there is smoke —

LIZARD'S BROTHER: There is fire!

ANIMALS: *(Cheering.)* Hurrah! Fire!

COYOTE: Quiet, please. This smoke and fire belong to Thunder and Lightning.

ANIMALS: *(Moaning.)* Oh, no. . . not Thunder and Lightning!

MOUSE: We must get this fire and bring it to The People.

FROG: That will not be easy. They say an evil bird, Woswosim, guards the fire at night. She never sleeps.

WILDCAT: That is no problem. *(Mimes motions.)* I, Wildcat, will creep up on this evil bird and devour her!

DEER: The noise would wake Thunder and Lightning and their Three Daughters. You would never come back alive!

SNAKE: Wait! How about if I sneak up and bite Woswosim in the ankle?

DOG: You would be crushed when she fell on you. You would never come back alive!

CHIPMUNK: I know! I will face this giant bird.

FOX: You? You're a little teeny chipmunk!

CHIPMUNK: I know what I am! I am a chipmunk who plays the flute.

(CHIPMUNK takes out a flute and plays a sweet melody; animals sigh and swoon. SOUND CUE: "Song of the Embers" — see Appendix.)

SKUNK: Chipmunk can play her flute and make Woswosim fall asleep. That will give us a chance to take the fire!

(ANIMALS agree and LIGHTS DIM or OUT. PAUSE, then LIGHTS UP on THUNDER, LIGHTNING, and THREE DAUGHTERS who are asleep. WOSWOSIM stands guard over them, spreading her wings and pacing slowly to and fro.)

WOSWOSIM: I, Woswosim, am the fiercest bird in the sky! I am so strong that I never sleep! No one in the world can defeat me!

(ANIMALS — all but SKUNK — enter silently creeping and hiding themselves behind boulders. CHIPMUNK takes out flute and begins to play softly. SOUND CUE: "Song of the Embers.")

WOSWOSIM: *(Jumps up, alert.)* What sound is that?

(CHIPMUNK stops; other ANIMALS shrink back. After a pause, CHIPMUNK plays again.)

WOSWOSIM: *(Relaxes.)* Hmmm. Must be some kind of bird...

(As the music continues, WOSWOSIM sits, gets comfortable against a rock and falls asleep. CHIPMUNK stops playing and ANIMALS spring into action: MOUSE unties the THREE DAUGHTERS' aprons and takes their fire. She puts some fire in DOG'S ear, some in COYOTE'S mouth, and the rest in the flute and gives the flute to DEER, who is the swiftest runner. All of a sudden, Thunder, Lightning and THREE DAUGHTERS awaken.)

THUNDER & LIGHTNING: What is going on?

THREE DAUGHTERS: They've stolen our fire!

THUNDER, LIGHTNING & THREE DAUGHTERS: Thieves!

LIGHTNING: Woswosim, wake up!

(SOUND CUE: drums. The ANIMALS scatter across stage, ducking and covering, guarding their fire; WOSWOSIM stands in campfire, flapping his wings; THUNDER, LIGHTNING and THREE DAUGHTERS begin dancing, creating a big rainstorm with wind, hail, and lightning. SOUND CUE: thunder, lightning, rain, and wind. LIGHT CUE: lightning. THUNDER, LIGHTNING, THREE DAUGHTERS, and WOSWOSIM chase the ANIMALS and are about to catch up with them, SKUNK rushes into the fray and jumps between the ANIMALS and their pursuers.)

ALL: SKUNK!!!

(ALL freeze as SKUNK, facing THUNDER and the other pursuers, and throws forth her arms as if casting a net. SOUND CUE: air squeaking out of a balloon.)

NARRATOR: And she sent toward them a mighty blast of his own wind . . . a powerful wind all skunks command even to this day, when they battle a bigger foe.

(THUNDER, LIGHTNING, THREE DAUGHTERS and WOSWOSIM fall down, shrink back, coughing, rubbing eyes. At this point, if some of the actors will resume playing PEOPLE for the final scene, they can exit now to change costumes.)

THUNDER, LIGHTNING, THREE DAUGHTERS,
& WOSWOSIM: Stop!! Stop!!

SKUNK: I will stop only if you promise that after today, you must never try to take fire from The People.

THUNDER, LIGHTNING, THREE DAUGHTERS,
& WOSWOSIM: We promise!

SKUNK: Forever more, you must stay up in the sky and be thunder and lightning.

(THUNDER, LIGHTNING, THREE DAUGHTERS, AND WOSWOSIM exit or go to final places on the stage. LIGHTS UP on PEOPLE, standing now, looking up and excitedly pointing at the sky.)

NARRATOR: And so the animals returned to the world with fire, which they gave to The People.

(MUSIC: ANIMALS hand fire embers to PEOPLE, who thank them profusely. Optional SONG/DANCE for entire cast.)

(MUSIC FADES as ANIMALS creep, crawl, flutter, scamper off-stage right while PEOPLE place embers into their new campfire, then gather in a semicircle round the fire, lie down, and sleep as LIGHTS DIM and MUSIC ENDS.)

(LIGHTS OUT.)

THE END

APPENDIX A
Sets and Props

BOULDERS
Use cardboard boxes or Styrofoam — cut and shape to form boulders. Paint black, brown, or gray.

CAMPFIRE
Arrange several large stones in a circle and place some kindling sticks in the center. You can also make stones out of Styrofoam pieces painted black or gray.

EMBERS
Use rocks or Styrofoam pieces that can be easily held by the actors and paint them red and black.

A FEW CORNCOBS
Fresh, dried, or plastic corn

SPEAR OR CLUB
Shape and decorate a large stick or Styrofoam piece or use a plastic toy spear.

A FLUTE OF ANY KIND

3 APRONS
(see Costumes)

APPENDIX B
Costumes

Costume creation can be a class art project. There are many ways to construct masks and other costume pieces with students — the following are some easy-to-make suggestions. Whenever possible, have students decorate their own costumes.

MAIDU PEOPLE
Tunics, serape style, or smocks of plain brown cloth; bare feet or sandals. A serape is a Mexican costumes made of a long, rectangular piece of cloth with a slit cut in the center, width-wise, just large enough for the head to fit through.

TOYESKOM AND WOSWOSIM (BIRDS)
Headpieces: Tape feathers to plastic, over-the-crown headbands. Use clear tape and firmly wrap the tape around the feather stems, layering the feathers around the headband. You can also make headbands out of construction paper, and firmly staple feather stems to each, using 2–3 staples per feather.
Wings: Make colored fabric capes and affix feathers along the bottom of each cape by firmly basting the stems with needle and thread (tape or staples may prove unreliable).

THUNDER
Make a tunic, serape style, or smock of white cloth and paint with black rainclouds and glitter.

LIGHTNING
Make a tunic, serape style, of dark blue or black cloth and paint with white lightning bolts and glitter.

THREE DAUGHTERS
Make or buy plain white, dark blue, or black aprons and paint with rainclouds and/or lightning and glitter.

ANIMALS

Make or buy animal masks and colored tunics, smocks or capes as appropriate for each animal. Ears can be made by cutting them out of construction paper and taping them onto plastic, over-the-crown headbands or stapling them to headbands made of construction paper.

Tails can be made by braiding together scarves or fabric strips and securing each to the back of pants or shorts with safety pins (children enjoy learning to braid).

APPENDIX C
Sound and Music

Each of the following sound cues can be created with percussion instruments or music — either live or on CD or tape. Select an appropriate sound or music theme for each character or group of characters.

SOUND CUES

Toyeskom

Thunder & Lightning and Three Daughters

Woswosim

The Animals

Chipmunk's Song: "Song of the Embers" (see next page)

Rainstorm: Suggestion: drums, rainsticks or maracas, and a sheet of aluminum metal that can be shaken to produce a strong crackling sound.

Skunk: Blow up a balloon and let the air out slowly at first so that it squeaks loudly and then let the air out quickly to make a loud puttering noise.

Thunder & Co.'s exit: Can be the same as their entrance sound or music.

The Animals give embers to the People: Can be the same as the Animals' entrance sound or music.

Finale Dance (optional)

Song of the Embers

by L.E. McCullough

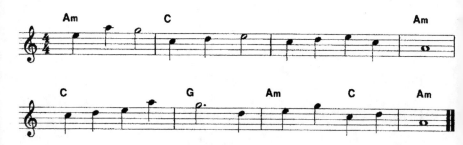

GLOSSARY

"The Big Lie" — the underlying imaginary premise that students must commit to holding as true when participating in a spontaneous role drama, improvisation, scene, or play

blocking — the planned movement and placement of actors on the stage

casting — choosing who will play which roles in a scene, play, or story dramatization

character — a person, animal, or other being in a story or play with distinguishing physical, vocal, and attitudinal characteristics. The actor's expression of these characteristics is known as "characterization."

choral speaking — a dramatic form in which a text is spoken, in unison or otherwise, by a group of participants

cinquain — a five-line poem, used in this curriculum in the following form:

noun

adjective, adjective

verb, verb, verb

phrase describing the above noun

same noun as above

climax — the highest point of tension in a story or play, in which the central conflicts have come to a head but have not yet been resolved

commitment — the strong intent to believe and engage in an imaginary situation; responding to the dramatic situation as if it were real

concentration — the ability to focus and keep one's attention fixed at will to the exclusion of internal or external distractions

context — the thematic framework within which a set of drama activities is presented, including an imaginary situation that motivates and links each of the activities

creative dramatics — "An improvisational, non-exhibitional, process-centered form of theater in which participants are guided by a leader to imagine, enact, and reflect upon human experiences." (as defined by the Children's Theater Association of America)

dialogue — words spoken by characters in a story or play, which may be written or improvised

divergent thinking — a form of thinking in which one allows ideas to spread in many directions from a single topic. Divergent thinking often results in unpredictable solutions to problems.

drama — from the Latin for *to do*; encompasses the form, concepts, and techniques involved in the expression of thought, feeling, character, and situation through body and voice, action and dialogue. Drama most often portrays or elucidates human experiences.

dramatic form — the form in which traditional works of drama are written, including the elements of exposition, rising action, climax, and resolution

dramatic tension — mental and emotional excitement in drama, born out of a situation of conflict which the audience or participants feel the need to have resolved

dramatization — writing or improvising a story or other piece of literature using elements of dramatic structure including character, action, and dialogue

exposition — the section of a drama, usually at the beginning, that introduces the primary characters and setting and provides the audience with the background information they will need in order to understand the drama's theme and the unfolding of its events

fluency — the ability to allow thought or action to flow, unimpeded by constraints

focus — the major point of attention, or the act of directing one's attention. Drama lessons have both an educational focus — the objectives for the lesson — and a dramatic focus, the imaginary situation created to capture and hold the students' attention.

generative art — art that is entirely original, created anew by the artist(s) — as opposed to "interpretive art"

General Space — the space of the entire room in which one is moving. Movement in General Space involves traveling through space.

gesture — an expressive movement of a part of the body that communicates an idea, a feeling, or an attitude

imagination — the process of creating a mental picture of something which is not currently present in physical reality

improvisation — the spontaneous creation and performance of action or dialogue in a dramatic form

in role — assuming a point of view in a role drama; also refers to a technique in drama education in which the teacher or other adult participates in a spontaneous role drama in order to heighten and advance the playing or to manage the students from within the drama

interpretive art — art in which the basic form (words, music, choreography, and so on) has already been created and that is then performed or otherwise interpreted by another artist or artists

kinesphere — the space one's own body takes up, which grows or shrinks depending on how far the limbs are stretched. Your kinesphere travels with you as you move.

Mantle of the Expert — a drama technique in which students work in role as experts with particular knowledge and skills that help them solve an imaginary problem or perform an imagined task. This technique helps students recognize the knowledge they already have while motivating them to expand their learning. This term was coined by Dorothy Heathcote, pioneer in this type of educational drama.

mirroring — a movement activity in which one or more people face a leader and copy his or her movements simultaneously

Movement Story — story narrated by the teacher while students move, the purpose of which is to guide students in developing body awareness and in exploring movement possibilities

pantomime — expressing an idea, feeling, intention, or situation through action without the use of the voice

reflection — thinking about the significance of an event or experience; becoming aware of one's own thoughts, feelings, or values

resolution — the section of a play or drama in which the conflict is resolved. This comes after the climax and is also known as the dénouement.

rising action — the introduction of characters and situations into a play or drama that create complications leading to the climax

ritual — a highly structured, symbolic activity that binds a group to a sense of shared meaning. In drama, use of ritual can encourage commitment to an imaginary situation.

role drama — a drama structure in which a series of events, based on one or more imaginary premises, unfolds spontaneously as participants improvise dialogue or action (see also **spontaneous role drama**)

Self Space — the space directly around one's body. When moving in Self Space, one does not travel.

setting — the physical location of a drama that may be expressed through backdrops, furniture, props, and so forth, or be completely imaginary. Setting sometimes also refers to the entire context of a drama including time period, situation, relationships between characters, and so on.

shadowing — a movement activity in which one or more people follow behind a leader's back and simultaneously imitate his or her movements through space

Sound Story — a story in which the teacher narrates and the students provide appropriate sounds

spectra of theater — the contrasts of Darkness/Light, Sound/Silence, Movement/Stillness, and The Expected/The Unexpected, used to create contrast and tension in a drama

spontaneous role drama — a drama structure in which a series of events, based on one or more imaginary premises, unfolds spontaneously as participants improvise dialogue or action (see also *role drama*)

stance — the position a teacher holds relative to the student when both teacher and student are in-role. Some basic stances possible for a teacher in role are: authority (leader, well above the level of students), facilitator (helper, slightly above the students), member (co-participant, on the same level as the students), and helpless one (needy, below level of students).

symbol — an object, word, or idea used as a focus for thought and feeling, or as a metaphor or representation of a larger idea. In drama, symbols provide a connection between the outer manifestation of a drama and the inner meaning of the experience for the participants.

tableau — a silent, motionless depiction of a scene or image through body position, facial expression, and grouping. Tableaux can be presented with or without props, costumes, or sets.

theater — dramatic performance for an audience that uses action and dialogue to tell a story or otherwise communicate ideas or arouse feelings. The term *theater* can also refer to the building in which such a performance takes place.

upgrade — to raise a drama to a higher level of formality or accuracy, or to deepen its level of significance. The upgrading of a drama may be accomplished through comments by the teacher that encourage reflection or provide accurate technical information, through the teacher's paraphrasing of students' language in a more formal or technically accurate form, or through the use of props that lend an air of professionalism or significance to a scene.

BIBLIOGRAPHY

Books about Child Development and Educational Theory

Ginsburg, Herbert and Sylvia Opper. 1979. *Piaget's Theory of Intellectual Development*. Englewood Cliffs, New Jersey: Prentice-Hall, Inc.

Gardner, Howard. 1983. *Frames of Mind*. New York: Basic Books, Inc.

Piaget, Jean and Barbel Inhelder. 1969. *The Psychology of the Child*. New York: Basic Books, Inc.

Books about Drama Education

ArtsConnection. 1995. *"Talent Identification Criteria in Theater Arts,"* Abstract. ArtsConnection.

Bolton, Gavin and Dorothy Heathcote. 1995. *Drama for Learning*. Portsmouth, N.H.: Heinemann, Inc.

Dunnington, Hazel Brain and Geraldine Brain Siks, editors. 1961. *Children's Theatre and Creative Dramatics*, Seattle, Wash.: University of Washington Press.

Gerke, Pamela and Helen Landalf. 1999. *Mail and Mystery, Family and Friends: Drama Curriculum for Second and Third Grades*. Lyme, N.H.: Smith and Kraus, Inc.

Johnstone, Keith. 1979. *Improv*. London: Faber and Faber, Ltd.

McCaslin, Nellie. 1996. *Creative Drama in the Classroom and Beyond*, Sixth Edition. New York: Longman Publishers.

McCaslin, Nellie. 1987. *Creative Drama in the Primary Grades*. New York: Longman, Inc.

Morgan, Norah and Juliana Saxton. 1976. *Teaching Drama*. Great Britain: Stanley Thornes Publishers, Ltd. *(Teaching Drama* must be ordered from England — but it's worth the cost if you are serious about studying role drama.)

Siks, Geraldine Brain. 1958. *Creative Dramatics: An Art for Children*. New York: Harper and Brothers.

Smith, Leisa, Project Director. 1995. *Arts Plus Theatre Curriculum Framework for Elementary Grades K–5*. Helena, Mont.: Helena Presents.

Spolin, Viola. 1986. *Theater Games for the Classroom*. Evanston, Ill.: Northwestern University Press.

Tarlington, Carole and Patrick Verriour. 1991. *Role Drama*. Portsmouth, N.H.: Heinemann Educational Books, Inc.

Wagner, Betty Jane. 1976. *Dorothy Heathcote / Drama as a Learning Medium*. Washington, D.C.: National Education Association. *Dorothy Heathcote / Drama as a Learning Medium* can be ordered through the National Education Association.

Way, Brian. 1967. *Development Through Drama*. Atlantic Highlands, N.J.: Humanities Press.

Wills, Barbara Salisbury. 1996. *Theatre Arts in the Elementary Classroom, Kindergarten Through Grade Three,* Second Edition. New Orleans, La.: Anchorage Press, Inc.

Literature for Dramatization

Day, Alexandra. 1996. *Good Dog Carl*. New York.: Little Simon Merchandise.

Fadiman, Clifton. 1984. *The World Treasury of Children's Literature, Books One and Two*. Boston: Little, Brown and Company.

Frey, Charles H. and John W. Griffith, editors. 1981. *Classics of Children's Literature*. New York: MacMillan Publishing Company, Inc.

Gerke, Pamela. 1996. *Multicultural Plays for Children Grades K–3* and *Grades 4–6* (two volumes). Lyme, N.H.: Smith and Kraus, Inc.

Haviland, Virginia (retold by). 1959–1995. *Favorite Fairy Tales Told in* _____ (series). Boston: Little, Brown, and Company.

Landalf, Helen. 1998. *The Secret Night World of Cats*. Lyme, N.H.: Smith and Kraus, Inc.

McCullough, L.E. 1996. "How the People Got Fire," *Plays of America from American Folklore*. Lyme, N.H.: Smith and Kraus, Inc.

Martin, Bill Jr. and Eric Carle. 1992. *Brown Bear, Brown Bear, What Do You See?* New York: Henry Holt.

Martin, Bill Jr. and Eric Carle. 1997. *Polar Bear, Polar Bear, What Do You Hear?* New York: Henry Holt.

Siks, Geraldine Brain. 1964. *Children's Literature for Dramatization*. New York: Harper and Row.

Suess, Dr. 1950. *If I Ran the Zoo*. New York: Random House.

Thistle, Louise. 1998. *Dramatizing Mother Goose*. Lyme, N.H.: Smith and Kraus, Inc.

Turkle, Brinton. 1976. *Deep in the Forest*. New York: The Trumpet Club.

Waddell, Martin, illustrated by Patrick Benson. 1992. *Owl Babies*. Cambridge, Mass.: Candlewick Press.

Ward, Winifred. 1952. *Stories to Dramatize*. Anchorage, Ky.: The Children's Theatre Press.

Williams, Sue, illustrated by Julie Vivas. 1989. *I Went Walking*. New York: The Trumpet Club.

Books about Creative Movement and Dance

Gilbert, Anne Green. 1977. *Teaching the Three R's Through Movement Experiences*. Minneapolis, Minn.: Burgess Publishing Company.

Gilbert, Anne Green. 1992. *Creative Dance for All Ages*. Reston, Va.: American Alliance for Health, Physical Education, Recreation and Dance.

Landalf, Helen and Pamela Gerke. 1996. *Movement Stories for Children*. Lyme, N.H.: Smith and Kraus, Inc.

Landalf, Helen. 1997. *Moving the Earth: Teaching Earth Science Through Movement in Grades 3–6*. Lyme, N.H., Smith and Kraus, Inc.

Landalf, Helen. 1998. *Moving is Relating: Teaching Interpersonal Skills Through Movement in Grades 3–6*. Lyme, N.H.: Smith and Kraus, Inc.

Morningstar, Moira. 1986. *Growing With Dance*. Heriot Bay, B.C.: Windborne Publications.

Also Recommended

Smith & Kraus, Inc. "Young Actor's Series" includes many books of monologues, scenes, and plays for children. To receive a current catalog call 800-895-4331, e-mail SandK@sover.net, or write:

Smith and Kraus, Inc. PO Box 127, Lyme, N.H. 03768

DISCOGRAPHY

Most of the drama lessons in this book can be presented without music. However, music often motivates self-expression and reduces self-consciousness in children. Several lessons in this book include suggestions for specific musical selections that are listed here, followed by other musical selections that you may find useful for drama and movement activities in general. These have been divided into two general types — active and energetic, and peaceful and relaxing — to help you determine which selections might be suitable for a particular activity.

Selections Suggested in the K–1 Drama Curriculum Lessons:

Lesson 1:

Barlin, Anne, "Freeze and Move," *Hello Toes: Movement Games for Children*, Princeton Book Company. (short selections of rhythms from different cultures)

Chappelle, Eric, "Chirpa, Chirpa," *Music for Creative Dance: Contrast and Continuum, Volume I*, Ravenna Ventures, Inc., RVCD 9301

Palmer, Hap "Pause," *Movin,'* Educational Activities, Inc., CD 546

Lesson 2:

Barlin, Anne, "Freeze and Move" *Hello Toes: Movement Games for Children*, Princeton Book Company. (short selections of rhythms from different cultures)

Chappelle, Eric, "Adagio for Two Violins," *Music for Creative Dance: Contrast and Continuum, Volume I,* Ravenna Ventures, Inc., RVCD 9301

Chappelle, Eric, "Chirpa, Chirpa", *Music for Creative Dance: Contrast and Continuum, Volume I,* Ravenna Ventures, Inc., RVCD 9301

Palmer, Hap, "Pause", *Movin,'* Educational Activities, Inc., CD 546

Palmer, Hap, *Seagulls*, (any selection), Educational Activities, Inc., CD 584

Shadowfax, "Dreams of Children," *Dreams of Children*, Windham Hill Records, WD-1038

Lesson 3:

Barlin, Anne, "Freeze and Move" *Hello Toes: Movement Games for Children*, Princeton Book Company. (short selections of rhythms from different cultures)

Chappelle, Eric, "Adagio for Two Violins," *Music for Creative Dance: Contrast and Continuum, Volume I,* Ravenna Ventures, Inc., RVCD 9301

Chappelle, Eric, "Chirpa, Chirpa", *Music for Creative Dance: Contrast and Continuum, Volume I,* Ravenna Ventures, Inc., RVCD 9301

Chappelle, Eric, "Pastarole," *Music for Creative Dance: Contrast and Continuum, Volume II,* Ravenna Ventures, Inc., RVCD 9401

Palmer, Hap, "Enter Sunlight," "Pause," "Twilight," *Movin', Movin,'* Educational Activities, Inc., CD 546

Lesson 12:

Greig, Edward, "In the Hall of the Mountain King," *Peer Gynt,* Angel 4XS-36531

Palmer, Hap, "Changes," *Getting to Know Myself,* Educational Activities, Inc., AC543

Lesson 16:

John, Esther "Little Dove," "Ocean Bossa," *The Elements, Volume II* (see ordering information at end of Discography)

Chappelle, Eric, "Dancing Digits," *Music for Creative Dance: Contrast and Continuum: Volume III.* Ravenna Ventures, Inc., RVCD 9801

Other Selections for Drama and Movement Activities

Active, Energetic

Day Parts, "Morning Blend," *Sunday Morning Coffee,* American Gramaphone Records, AGCD100

Dead Can Dance, "Bird," *A Passage in Time,* Ryko, RCD 20215

Penguin Café Orchestra, *Broadcasting From Home* (any selection), Editions EG, EGEDC38

Roth, Gabrielle and the Mirrors, *Totem* (any selection), Raven Recording, LC5565

Peaceful, Relaxing

Day Parts, "Across the View," *Sunday Morning Coffee*, American Gramaphone
  Records, AGCD100
Enya, "Caribbean Blue," *Shepherd Moons*, Reprise Records, 4-26775
Nakai, Carlos R., *Earth Spirit* (any selection), Canyon Records, CR-612
  Volume 4
Vollenweider, Andreas, "The Glass Hall," *White Winds*, CBS FMT 39963

Recommended Collections

- Chappelle, Eric, *Music for Creative Dance: Contrast and Continuum,
  Volumes I, II and III,* Ravenna Ventures, Inc., RVCD 9301, 9401 and 9801
  These three CDs contain many selections with pauses and alternating
  phrases, and they are excellent for use in exploring movement. Each CD
  comes with a booklet of Creative Dance teaching ideas.

    To order, call or write:
    Ravenna Ventures, Inc.   *(206) 528 . 1556*
    4756 University Village Pl. NE. #117
    Seattle, WA. 98105

- John, Esther "Little Dove," *The Elements, Volumes I and II* Instrumental
  music evoking the elements of earth, air, fire, and water

    To order, write:
    Esther "Little Dove" John and the Mission for Music and Healing
    c/o Church Council of Greater Seattle
    4759 15th Ave. N.E.
    Seattle, WA. 98105

- *Classical Cats*, Zanicorn Entertainment, Ltd. ZA01 This is a delightful collection of classical pieces by a variety of composers.

- *One World*, Putamayo World Music, ISBN 1-885265-36-0. This CD is a
  sampler of music from many cultures, including African, South American,
  and European. Putamayo World Music also offers other multicultural col-
  lections.

Other Smith and Kraus Books
by Pamela Gerke
and Helen Landalf

Multicultural Plays for Children, Grades K–3

Multicultural Plays for Children, Grades 4–6

Movement Stories for Children, Ages 3–6

Moving the Earth: Teaching Earth Science
through Movement, Grades 3–6

Moving is Relating: Developing Interpersonal Skills
through Movement, Grades 3–6

Mail and Mystery, Family and Friends:
Drama Curriculum for Second and Third Grades

ABOUT THE AUTHORS

HELEN LANDALF attended the State University of New York at Purchase as a member of the Professional Actor's Training Program, then graduated from the University of Washington in Seattle with a B.A. in Theater Arts and a K–12 Teaching Certification. Helen has performed as both an actress and a dancer, and she currently teaches Creative and Modern Dance for children at the Creative Dance Center in Seattle. She has served as an Artist in Residence for the Montana Public Schools, and she frequently presents workshops for classroom teachers on integrating dance into the basic curriculum. Helen is author of a children's book, *The Secret Night World of Cats*, illustrated by her brother Mark Rimland, *Movement Stories for Children* with Pamela Gerke, *Moving the Earth: Teaching Earth Science Through Movement in Grades 3–6*, and *Moving is Relating: Teaching Interpersonal Skills Through Movement in Grades 3–6*, all published by Smith and Kraus, Inc.

PAMELA GERKE received her B.A. in English from the University of California at Berkeley and a Multiple Subjects Teaching Credential from Pacific Oaks College in Pasadena, California. She is Artistic Director and Playwright for Kids Action Theater in Seattle, since founding the program in 1988. She has written and/or directed over thirty children's plays. She is also a composer, arranger and conductor for several other shows and for choirs. Pamela is author of *Multicultural Plays for Children, Grades K–6* (in 2 volumes), and *Movement Stories for Children* with Helen Landalf, both published by Smith and Kraus, Inc. She is also the creator of *Doors to Rewards*, a creative reward system for children published by Western Psychological Services. Pamela currently divides her time between Kids Action Theater, arts in education residencies, and composing or arranging music for plays and choirs.